"Barbara Bissonnette's book is a must-read for those with Asperger's Syndrome preparing to enter the workforce or who are struggling in their jobs. It provides a comprehensive, well-organized wealth of knowledge about areas of possible workplace challenge along with concrete, practical coping strategies for successful employment. Most importantly, Barbara writes from a respectful, compassionate, non-judgmental viewpoint, weaving in real-life workplace stories gleaned from her years of successful coaching. Her message is one of hope and encouragement. In addition to providing invaluable information and practical advice for individuals on the autism spectrum, *Asperger's Syndrome Workplace Survival Guide* is an essential reference book for parents and professionals and should be required reading for every job coach and Vocational Rehabilitation counselor."

—*Brenda Weitzberg, Executive Director, Aspiritech*

"This is a one-of-a-kind resource that is equally useful to adults on the spectrum and neurotypical employers. Bissonnette very artfully uses her years of experience as an NT employer to offer detailed and practical 'inside information' to the reader with AS, and does so with a voice that is genuinely sensitive. She is honest while respectful, encouraging without patronizing. This is going on my must-read list for my patients. Well done!"

—*Valerie L. Gaus, Ph.D., psychologist in private practice*

"Understanding Asperger's Syndrome itself is a pre-requisite for someone with AS; understanding exactly how it impacts in a real-life work context is quite another matter. *Asperger's Syndrome Workplace Survival Guide* overcomes this by providing the understanding and tools that a person with Asperger's needs in the workplace and explaining the rules of employment that can appear so alien. It is the perfect guide for surviving and thriving in the world of work!"

—*Malcolm Johnson, author of* Managing with Asperger Syndrome

"Ever had a toolkit that had just the right tools you needed for a range of jobs? That's the feeling you get reading *Asperger's Syndrome Workplace Survival Guide*. Barbara's real-world examples and tactics will help people with Asperger's Syndrome land and hold jobs. It's also a great resource to help companies tap a pool of exceptional talent."

—*Dan Coulter, author of* Life in the Asperger Lane *and co-founder of Coulter Video*

"Barbara Bissonnette's book is loaded with common-sense, no-punches-pulled direct action examples of interventions by a personal coach intimately familiar with the real world of work and empathetic to the different workings of the ASD mind… It not only preaches the gospel of success but also explains employment failure warning signs and provides ASD adults with multiple pathways to high-grade, professionally proven changes in behavior and attitudes likely to assure individual success in the workplace."

—*Roger N. Meyer, author of* Asperger Syndrome Employment Workbook

ASPERGER'S SYNDROME WORKPLACE SURVIVAL GUIDE

A Neurotypical's Secrets for Success

BARBARA BISSONNETTE

Foreword by Yvona Fast

Jessica Kingsley *Publishers*
London and Philadelphia

Rationality of Beliefs Checklist on pages 123–124
reproduced with kind permission from Lewis R. Stern.

This edition published in 2013
by Jessica Kingsley Publishers
116 Pentonville Road
London N1 9JB, UK
and
400 Market Street, Suite 400
Philadelphia, PA 19106, USA

www.jkp.com

First published in 2010 by Forward Motion Coaching

Library of Congress Cataloging in Publication Data
A CIP catalog record for this book is available from the Library of Congress

British Library Cataloguing in Publication Data
A CIP catalogue record for this book is available from the British Library

ISBN 978 1 84905 943 5
eISBN 978 0 85700 807 7

Printed and bound in the USA

This book is dedicated to the men and women with Asperger's Syndrome and Nonverbal Learning Disorder who I have had the privilege to know and to coach. Thank you for all that you have taught me.

To Anna S., whose hard work and refusal to give up truly is an inspiration.

To Ellen Korin for her encouragement, mentoring and friendship.

To my husband Michael for his love and support.

CONTENTS

FOREWORD BY YVONA FAST 11

1 WHAT DOES IT TAKE TO MAKE IT IN THE NT
  WORKPLACE, ANYWAY? 13
  How to Use This Book to Develop and Make Changes 17

2 A PRIMER ON COMMUNICATION AT WORK . . . 20
  Meaning Comes from Context 22
  Most Communication is Nonverbal 25

3 MAKING THE RIGHT FIRST IMPRESSION AND
  FITTING IN 30
  How to Introduce Yourself to Co-Workers 33
  Using Small Talk to Build Relationships 34
  How to Make a Reasonable Amount of Small Talk 35
  Anatomy of a Welcome Lunch 37
  Why You Need a Work Buddy 40
  Asking for Help is a Good Thing; *Being* Too Helpful is Not 43
  How to Be a Team Player 46
  Meeting Employer Expectations 49
  Strategies for Clarifying Expectations 53
  Projecting Confidence 57

4 PEOPLE SKILLS 61
  Accepting Feedback and Criticism 62
  Being Critical of Others 64
  Dealing with Authority 65
  Dealing with Change 68
  Conflicts and Disagreements 72
  Conflict...or Misunderstanding? 77
  A Primer on Office Politics 78
  Office Politics in Action 80
  What if Things Get Ugly? 85

5   EXECUTIVE FUNCTIONS AT WORK: MANAGING
     TIME AND GETTING THINGS DONE. 86
     Working Memory and Multitasking.   87
     Managing Time.   89
     Planning Projects.   94
     Getting to the Point: Right-Sizing Communications.   100
     Being Flexible and Seeing Options   103
     Setting Realistic Goals.   106
     Creating an Action Plan that Works.   110

6   MANAGING ANGER, FRUSTRATION,
     ANXIETY, AND STRESS. .115
     Put the Actions of Others into Perspective.   119
     How to Change Distorted Thinking Patterns   122
     Managing Anxiety.   125
     More Anxiety Management Strategies   129
     Sensory Issues on the Job.   130
     Bullying and Harassment at Work.   134
     What to Do if You Are Bullied or Harassed.   138

7   MANAGING YOUR CAREER. 141
     Build on Your Strengths.   142
     Accept Your Limitations   145
     How to Tell if You Are in the Wrong Job or Career   150
     Should You Be a Manager?   152
     Performing a SWOT Analysis   155
     Why You Need to Network, Even When You're Employed   160
     Professional Associations.   162
     More Ways to Network.   163
     Anatomy of a 30-Second Elevator Speech   164
     What to Do if You Are Fired   165
     What Not to Do if You Are Fired.   168
     How to Resign.   169

8   DISCLOSURE AND
     ACCOMMODATIONS 172
     Disclosing in a Solution-Focused Way   175
     Dos and Don'ts of Disclosing   183
     Examples of Disclosure Strategies   185

9   IN THE FINAL ANALYSIS 188

APPENDIX: ASPERGER'S SYNDROME GUIDE
FOR EMPLOYERS   191
Common Workplace Challenges.   193
Communication Challenges   193
Organizational Challenges   194
Sensory and Motor Challenges   195
Optimal Jobs and Work Environments.   196
Working with People Who Have Asperger's Syndrome   197

REFERENCES   200

FURTHER READING   202

ABOUT THE AUTHOR   203

INDEX.   204

FOREWORD

I consider it a privilege to write the foreword to *Asperger's Syndrome Workplace Survival Guide.* Barbara has been helping individuals on the spectrum obtain and maintain employment for many years.

Sigmund Freud said that everyone wants to work and to love—and people on the autism spectrum are no exception. Work is not just a means to earn money to supply our needs and wants. Work is how we contribute to our communities, how people see us as valuable, productive citizens of society.

Individuals on the autism spectrum have many wonderful characteristics that can be useful in the right work environment. As a group, we tend to be articulate, thorough, kind, and persistent. Many of us are highly educated, have great verbal and writing skills, and are highly motivated, conscientious, honest, and hardworking. In spite of this, it can be difficult to find the job that will make allowances and accommodations for our disabilities while making our abilities shine.

Those on the autism spectrum who find a career that allows them to thrive are the lucky few. According to the Social Security Administration, only about 6 percent of adults with autism work full time. The majority are unemployed or under-employed. It is appalling that so many intelligent, educated, honest, hardworking folks are unable to find or maintain meaningful employment. And to extend that figure to 85 percent of a given population shows something is wrong with the system.

Barbara Bissonnette is working to change that. Over the past years, she has coached individuals with Asperger's Syndrome and Nonverbal Learning Disorder on a range of issues related to work and career. She has a lot of experience assisting those on the spectrum in finding and maintaining fulfilling careers.

Barbara understands that everyone has unique gifts that they bring to the world and the workplace. People on the autism spectrum can do a variety of jobs, from highly technical to creative. She recognizes that individuals on the spectrum vary widely in their abilities, challenges, and communication styles. Some are awkward in their interactions, while others are charming and talkative but may alienate others with blunt comments or social gaffes.

Barbara understands that finding a career we can thrive in doesn't happen by chance. It requires planning and hard work. It entails understanding our strengths and how to best use them on the job.

There's a lot in this book that I wish I had known when I began planning my own career path. I thought my difficulties were due to poor self-esteem and incompetence, though I couldn't quite pinpoint why. After decades of struggle to establish a career and understand my unique mind, I learned that I had Nonverbal Learning Disorder. By then I was 42 years old, and years of repeated trying, failing, and not understanding what was going on had taken their toll.

My story is typical of many on the spectrum. We go through life pretending to be normal, trying to fit into a world that refuses to accept us. Most often, we are accused of being lazy or rude when in fact most of us work very hard to achieve—and yet all our effort and persistence is not good enough for the neurotypical world we live in. People don't understand how someone who seems so "normal" or "bright" has such problems with certain "simple" things.

Barbara's book would have explained to me how spectrumites and neurotypicals can clash in workplace environments due to differences in communication styles, learning styles, social interaction, and physical needs—things I was unaware of. From making the right first impression to being a team player and fitting in, Barbara guides the reader through the minefields of working in the foreign neurotypical culture. With her help, individuals on the spectrum can become useful to an organization, gain respect from their colleagues for their unique contributions, and begin to feel a sense of belonging.

This book addresses those on the spectrum seeking employment, but will also benefit career counselors, employers hiring those on the spectrum, and anyone who wants to understand people on the spectrum and help them fit into the workplace culture.

Yvona Fast

Support Groups Manager, GRASP, and author of Employment for Individuals with Asperger Syndrome or Non-Verbal Learning Disability: Stories and Strategies

CHAPTER 1

WHAT DOES IT TAKE TO MAKE IT IN THE NT WORKPLACE, ANYWAY?

I am not aware of any reliable employment statistics for adults with Asperger's Syndrome (AS). An often-quoted statistic is that 85 percent are either un- or under-employed. Whether that number is accurate or not, clearly there are too many intelligent, talented, college-educated individuals who are not able to fully utilize their talents in the workplace.

Kevin summed up a big part of the problem. He was crushed after losing his first post-college job in just six weeks. "At school, it was about getting good grades," he said, "at work, it's about figuring out what people want."

If you are a person who has Asperger's Syndrome, like Kevin, figuring out what people want probably seems like an impossible task. No matter how hard you try, you just don't "get it" like everyone else. At work, people can say one thing but mean another. They accuse you of not listening, yet won't explain exactly what they want from you. When you guess, you usually guess wrong.

It is exhausting to be anxious every day about saying or doing the wrong thing. You want to interact with your co-workers, but don't know what to say. Sometimes, their conversations seem so trivial or boring that you don't even try to join in. Other times, you think that you're being friendly and helpful, but are accused of being "rude" or "hard to get along with." Why all the emphasis on socializing, anyway? What is more important: chatting in the lunch room or getting your work done?

Speaking of getting your work done, the continual interruptions make it so hard to concentrate! You lose track of what you were doing, or forget altogether. The pressure starts to mount. You're getting confused. Soon, you become paralyzed. You are not sure what you should be doing, so you abandon the current project and return to an earlier task. Later, your supervisor says that you need to prioritize better.

On top of all this, you are assaulted by sights, sounds, smells, and textures that are uncomfortable (even torturous) and that no one else seems to notice. Why can't people turn down the lights, be quiet, and stop eating noxious-smelling food at their desks?

It is all very frustrating, and sometimes makes you really angry, particularly if you have been fired once, or more than once, or many more times than once and you don't really know what went wrong. What are you supposed to do differently now? It keeps getting harder to explain the employment gaps and short-term jobs on your resume. You shouldn't lie, but if you tell the full truth, no one will want to hire you.

Perhaps you are employed, but struggle to carry out job duties, or are bored in a position that doesn't make use of your talents or intellect. Maybe you have earned a promotion because of your excellent work; you now are required to show "leadership" and have no idea what to do. Or, worst of all, a new supervisor has changed all the rules leaving you frantically trying to figure out what is expected of you now.

At times, you wonder whether you should disclose your Asperger's Syndrome to your employer. Technically, there is legislation (such as the Americans with Disabilities Act in the United States) which protects people from discrimination, but this is the real world. It is hard to predict how your manager will react, and proving discrimination can be difficult, time consuming, and expensive. Still, disclosure means that you can request accommodations, which you are certain would enable you to improve your performance.

If you can relate to any or all of the above, then you have a lot in common with the clients in my coaching practice. They are men and women who, like you, are smart and skilled. Most have college degrees, and some have Masters' degrees or doctorates. They are young people who are just entering the workforce, and individuals in their 30s, 40s, 50s, and even 60s who have spent years in the workforce.

Although they have been diagnosed with Asperger's Syndrome, or strongly suspect that they have it, each client is very different. For some, holding on to *any* job is a significant challenge. Others maintain steady employment, and some get promoted, but struggle to understand expectations and communicate with co-workers. Even those who are earning six-figure salaries have difficulty interacting with colleagues.

My clients seek coaching to discover what career they will like and be successful at, to learn how to interview, and to maintain employment. They want techniques for managing their time and prioritizing projects. They want to know how to address performance problems, and figure out whether to disclose. All are eager to learn just what it is that NTs want. (NT stands for neurotypical, meaning a person who is not on the autism spectrum.)

As a neurotypical, I act as a bridge between my clients and their co-workers. Prior to starting my coaching practice, I spent 20 years in the business world. I hired staff, managed departments, launched new products, and increased sales.

My introduction to Asperger's Syndrome happened by accident. In the spring of 2006, I was midway through a graduate certificate program in executive coaching from the Massachusetts School of Professional Psychology (MSPP). Four years earlier, I had quit my job as Vice President of Marketing and Sales, and then consulted part-time with that company, while testing the waters of professional coaching. I was looking for a way to give back my business experience to people who could benefit the most from it. Coaching entrepreneurs and small business owners seemed the ideal way to do that.

Thumbing through the MSPP continuing education catalog, I noticed a workshop about coaching people with Asperger's Syndrome. It sounded interesting so I gave myself permission to take a Friday morning off to attend. I spent the better part of four hours that Friday literally on the edge of my chair. What I heard was fascinating and familiar. I was certain that during my corporate career I had worked with people who had Asperger's Syndrome. A few weeks later, I met with the executive director of the Asperger's Association of New England. She asked a question that changed everything: "Have you thought about coaching people with Asperger's?"

Could I? I began learning about Asperger's Syndrome by reading books, visiting websites, and talking to professionals such as educators, advocates, psychotherapists and neuropsychologists. I attended workshops and conferences. I talked to more professionals. My idea was to specialize in career development coaching for adults. It was met with enthusiasm by these professionals. "No one is doing that," I heard, again and again. Finally, I had found a group of people who could benefit from my business experience.

Today, I coach individuals with Asperger's Syndrome and Nonverbal Learning Disorder on a range of issues related to work and career. The coaching process requires my clients learn and practice new skills, take action toward a goal, and be willing to experiment. It is not about changing *who you are* as a person; it is about changing *how you approach* situations and interact with others, so that you can function more effectively at work. It can be about finding a job that capitalizes on your strengths, while discovering ways to minimize or work around your limitations.

In this book, you will learn about the techniques that I use with my clients. I'll share information about how to get along with your co-workers, clarify expectations with your supervisor, and handle specific problems. Since I believe that it is easier to learn from examples, I have included many from my client cases. In order to protect people's privacy, names and identifying details have been changed, and composites have been used.

My perspective as a neurotypical business person will help you navigate the workplace and "fit in." This means being able to interact with co-workers in a way that makes them feel comfortable working with you.

Sometimes I am asked why NTs are so "mean," or why Aspergians have to do all of the changing. "Just because I'm not a social person, it doesn't mean that I'm a bad person," one man said. NTs aren't intentionally mean. They just have a very limited understanding of Asperger's Syndrome. Myths and misconceptions abound. I still meet NTs who think that everyone with Asperger's is a genius, or is working in the information technology industry. Many believe the stereotype of the loner who "doesn't like people," and who isn't empathic. Some think that Asperger's Syndrome is a personality problem.

In a workplace dominated by neurotypicals, this lack of understanding results in communication gaffes being treated as attitude or behavior problems. Difficulty with executive functioning is interpreted as lack of effort or a disregard for doing a good job. The individual who is sensitive to light, odors or sounds is viewed as demanding and picky.

Should it be like this? No. Will it change overnight? No. Will it change someday? Yes. But what do you do in the meantime?

Choose a career wisely, based on your interests and strengths. Learn how to communicate *well enough* to get along with co-workers. Be open to new ways of doing things. Ask NTs for help (they are everywhere, so why not use them?!). Do not allow bad experiences from the past to make you angry and bitter. Instead, think about how you want people to perceive you.

Remember, *everyone* has to fit into cultural expectations and norms. During my corporate career, there were times that I had to work with people whom I didn't like, adhere to policies that I thought were silly, and settle for doing work that was good enough, instead of outstanding. I experienced periods of boredom, uncertainty, and frustration. I found some senior executives thoroughly intimidating. No job is perfect, but you probably get a regular paycheck, paid vacation and sick time, and health insurance if you live in the U.S.

This is not to minimize in any way the very real challenges that the majority of people with Asperger's Syndrome face at work. It is to let you know that whenever groups of people get together, there will be conflicts, power struggles and frustrations. Neurotypicals have problems on the job, too.

HOW TO USE THIS BOOK TO DEVELOP AND MAKE CHANGES

The content of this book is based on the situations that I see again and again in my coaching practice. Not every chapter will apply to you, but many of them will. My intention is to offer specific techniques that you can use to address various circumstances. If you are just entering the workforce, this book will help you understand what employers expect from you, and show you how to avoid some of the common problems that occur.

This first chapter has provided an overview of the challenges that many people with Asperger's Syndrome face in the workplace.

Chapter 2 is a primer on interpersonal communication. It is my experience that communication causes most of the problems people with Asperger's Syndrome have at work. This is because communication problems often appear to be attitude or behavior problems. This chapter explains the importance of situational context and nonverbal cues for understanding the real meaning of what someone says.

Chapter 3 focuses on the elusive concept of "fitting in." As I will stress throughout this book, technical skill is not the primary factor in employment success. It is the ability to work with other people. This does not mean that you must be friends with your co-workers, or even like them. What you need to do is act in ways that enable others to work effectively with you. This involves establishing good relationships with your colleagues, asking for help when you need it, working as a member of a team, and meeting expectations for productivity and job performance.

The people skills discussed in Chapter 4 are necessary for navigating the complexities of social interaction in the workplace. You will interact with individuals who have different personalities, backgrounds, goals and styles of working. You will receive feedback, which may include criticism of certain aspects of your performance. There will be disagreements and conflicts that must be addressed, so that they do not interfere with productivity. And although *everyone* dislikes office politics, it is part of the inner workings of every organization.

Chapter 5 is about planning projects, managing time, being flexible, and setting realistic goals. In other words: getting your work done on time! You will learn what it really means to multitask, how to improve your short-term memory, plan how long tasks will take, and produce clear written and verbal communications.

In order to maintain employment, it is essential that you cope with stress, and manage strong emotions such as anger and anxiety. When you are emotionally upset, you are literally not thinking clearly, and may say or do things that can damage your reputation, or cost you your job. Chapter 6 explains why this is so, and offers numerous strategies for avoiding meltdowns and burnout.

In the next chapter, career management topics are addressed. They are applicable no matter what kind of career or job you have. When I think about clients who are the most successful, what they have in common is knowledge of their strengths and limitations. They use this information to make better job choices, and to recognize when they are in the wrong position. This chapter also includes information about networking, which is an important activity even when you are employed. It also discusses how to leave a company— voluntarily or not—on the best terms possible.

Disclosure and accommodations are the focus of Chapter 8. For some of my clients, accommodations have meant the difference between losing a job and keeping it. There is an overview of the Americans with Disabilities Act that explains key terms such as *essential job functions*, *undue hardship*, and *reasonable accommodation*. The pros and cons of disclosing at various stages of the employment cycle are discussed. You will learn how to develop a disclosure strategy that increases the chances of receiving the modifications that you need.

You are probably pretty tired of having to do all of the adjusting to fit into the neurotypical workplace. Some innovative organizations are creating jobs that take advantage of the specialized skills of individuals with Asperger's Syndrome. In Chapter 9, I will describe these models, and share some final thoughts about Asperger's Syndrome and employment.

Read through the book and decide what changes you need to make. Choose one or two areas to focus on at a time. Trying to make too many changes at once is overwhelming and won't work very well. You might need help from a neurotypical who can translate some of the techniques into a plan that addresses your specific needs. This person can be a professional coach or psychotherapist, or someone in your personal life who you trust. Perhaps there is a colleague at work who is friendly and supportive, and can help you put some of the changes into action.

Action is the key when you want to make a change. Usually, it is the small, consistent steps taken over time that get big results. You don't have to do everything perfectly, either. It takes practice to master a new skill. The most successful clients I work with are those who are willing to practice new attitudes or behaviors, even though they initially feel uncomfortable. The more they practice, the easier the new way becomes.

Motivation is a factor when you are making changes. The best way to maintain your focus and determination over an extended period of time is to set a meaningful goal. Sometimes, the primary motivator for change at work is fear—usually of job loss. Even if this is your impetus, try to put it in the context of a larger, more positive goal. For instance, you may decide that your greater goal is to improve your communication skills, or ability to handle frustration, so that you are better able to handle daily situations.

Experiment with change. Decide what you will do differently, try it for a reasonable amount of time, and assess the results. Two to three weeks is a realistic experimental period. If the change isn't working, figure out why, or what else you can try.

Do not give up. I have worked with clients who tell me that they absolutely, positively, in no way, can never, *e-v-e-r* do something…and a few months later, they are doing it! If you find yourself becoming discouraged, seek out support. Difficulties in the workplace are not exclusive to people with Asperger's Syndrome. Plenty of neurotypicals get fired, passed up for promotions, receive disciplinary action or realize that they are in the wrong career. The key is to learn from your experiences and be willing to change.

CHAPTER 2

A PRIMER ON COMMUNICATION AT WORK

"Social skills are the key to success in life. Lack of them will cost you everything—friends, lovers and a career in something you love." (Industrial Hygienist, age 50)

When I speak to organizations about Asperger's Syndrome, I explain it as a fundamental difference in the hardwiring of the brain. Neurotypicals, I say, orient themselves to other people, while Aspergians focus on facts and information. This does not mean that a person with Asperger's Syndrome doesn't *want* to have relationships with others. It is quite the contrary. However, initiating and maintaining these relationships is difficult. The interpersonal communication skills that NTs learn intuitively must be learned intellectually by Aspergians. This is difficult, time consuming, and exhausting.

It is my estimate that problems with interpersonal communication account for 80 percent of the difficulties that people with Asperger's Syndrome have in the workplace. To neurotypicals, the communication problems of Aspergians appear to be attitude or behavior problems, and are treated accordingly. This is not because NTs are insensitive or mean. It is because they are unaware that some people do not develop this intuitive social understanding, and are unable to adapt their behavior.

Neurotypicals place a high value on interpersonal relationships at work. In a survey of the top skills and personal qualities that employers want from employees, the ability to work in a team was ranked number one, followed by strong verbal communication skills, and decision-making and problem-solving. Technical knowledge was ranked seventh (NACE 2011). I have seen many other surveys showing the correlation between satisfaction at work and the quality of relationships with supervisors and co-workers.

Interpersonal relationships even play a role in who is hired, fired, and promoted. Employers evaluate job candidates on their education, skills, experience, *and* their ability to work with other people. Several times during my corporate career, I was involved in decisions about layoffs. Presuming that two people were meeting performance expectations, the decision about who would stay was based on who got along better with co-workers. Similarly, when a choice was made about who would receive a promotion, invariably one of the final questions was, "Who do people like working with most?"

Work is a group endeavor. Even if you spend a large part of the day working by yourself, you still need to interact with your supervisor, and possibly co-workers, customers, or vendors. Self-employed individuals must manage relationships with customers, potential customers, and service providers, such as accountants and lawyers.

Developing your communication skills is the most important thing that you can do to maintain employment and manage your career. These skills enable you to interact effectively with others by:

- understanding employer expectations

- influencing how other people perceive you by working cooperatively

- sharing your ideas

- getting along with others.

Developing these skills is not about creating scripts, which are statements that are prepared in advance. Scripts can be useful for introducing yourself, initiating certain conversations, or explaining unexpected behaviors. However, they are insufficient for managing the complexity of human interaction in the workplace. It is not possible to anticipate and prepare a specific response for every interaction that might happen in a single day, never mind over the course of one's career!

Later chapters of this book provide specific recommendations for effective workplace communication. First, it will be helpful for you to understand a few basics about how neurotypicals communicate.

MEANING COMES FROM CONTEXT

"Mental exhaustion comes from having to figure things out cognitively rather than intuitively. If I seem 'slow,' it is because I have to deliberately think things through." (Web Content Administrator, age 42)

Sean had tried for months to land an entry-level information technology (IT) position. He was excited about the prospect of working at a small software firm. After successful interviews with the human resources manager and his potential supervisor, Sean returned to meet with two members of the IT department who had both worked in this field for more than a decade.

Sean listened as they described their roles at the company, and commented that their jobs sounded very simple. He was surprised when he received a phone call from the human resources manager telling him that his arrogance had cost him the job. "I figured that by telling them that their jobs were simple, they would see how smart I am and want to hire me."

Kevin's supervisor asked him to "take a look" at new scheduling software that the company had recently purchased. Two weeks later, the supervisor confronted Kevin, angrily inquiring why he wasn't using the software. "I took a look at it like you asked," Kevin explained, "but I didn't think it would be useful so I deleted it off my computer." Recalling the exchange during a coaching session, Kevin asked me, "If my boss wanted me to *use* the software, why didn't he just say so?"

If you have experienced similar miscommunication, each incident probably leaves you more confused, frustrated and anxious. In the examples of Sean and Kevin, words were spoken, but there was not clear communication. They responded to *words* they heard, without considering the situational context, and nonverbal signals (such as body language and vocal inflection) that reveal the real *meaning* of the words.

Pragmatics is defined as "the rules governing the use of language in social situations" (Fogle 2013, p.12). Figuring out the social rules of how to interact with others depends on the context of a situation, and the type of relationship you have with the person or persons to whom you are speaking (Fogle 2013).

Examples of good pragmatic ability include: speaking to the president of the company in a more formal way than you speak to your peers; adjusting the content of a presentation based on what your audience already knows, and needs to know, about a topic; noticing when people are bored and want to end the conversation; staying on topic during a meeting.

Sean didn't adjust his communication, as he should have, to fit in with two experienced professionals. As someone just entering the field, Sean appeared conceited and disrespectful by describing their jobs as "simple." Kevin focused only on his supervisor's words to "take a look at" the software. Later on, Kevin realized that he missed situational clues that revealed his supervisor's implied meaning. For example, every member of the department received the software, and Kevin was the only one who wasn't using it to schedule and track projects. Taken within this context, Kevin understood that what his boss was really communicating was, "We have purchased a new tool for everyone in the department to begin using."

To the degree that a person has trouble grasping situational context, he will struggle to say and do the "right" things. In his book, *Autism as Context Blindness*, Dr. Peter Vermeulen describes how neurotypicals are able to process contextual clues within a fraction of a second, largely subconsciously. In contrast, individuals on the autism spectrum must consciously think about context and how to respond, a process that takes time and mental effort (Vermeulen 2012).

Neurotypicals assume that everyone has an innate ability to size up people and situations quickly and accurately. This is why they communicate in ways that Aspergians find so confusing. NTs assume that you will figure out motives without being told, and know what is expected, based on inferences and previous experience. They will not explain situations or procedures that are considered obvious, or matters of common sense. They assess situations based on the gestalt, or big picture, instead of discrete details. Information about a current situation is integrated with memories of similar experiences, plus awareness of the other people involved, in order to draw conclusions, and decide what action to take. This is in sharp contrast to many Aspergians, who will probably identify with these words from a former client: "I have little or no accurate sense for what would be appropriate to any other given person, or to any situation that involves anyone other than me."

Suppose a staff member makes a mistake. The neurotypical manager will consider the severity of the error, the context in which it occurred, and the individual's previous performance. He will probably overlook a minor typo made by an employee with an excellent track record, especially if that person was working under a tight deadline. Contrast this with the more rigid, black-and-white thinking of a manager with Asperger's Syndrome. He may consider a mistake to be a mistake, and not hesitate to point it out.

Theory of mind is the ability to understand another person's perspective (Vermeulen 2012). People having strong theory of mind recognize that others have thoughts, desires, knowledge, feelings and motives that differ from their own. In order to recognize another person's mental state, and understand why he thinks or feels a certain way, they always consider the situational context (Vermeulen 2012).

The weaker your theory of mind, the more random and confusing the actions of other people will seem. Alice could not reconcile that her supervisor praised her outstanding programming skill, while also insisting that products be released with code that was not perfect. "Why won't he let me do good work?" she fumed. "It's a lie for the company to say that the products are top quality."

What Alice didn't recognize was that her supervisor was responsible for releasing products in time to meet quarterly sales targets and promised delivery schedules. From his perspective, the company's products *are* top quality because they out-sell competing brands and earn high ratings in the trade press and from customers. The supervisor is also aware that customers expect a certain number of imperfections in any piece of software. Alice's weak theory of mind ability prevented her from considering her supervisor's point of view, and, as a result, his decisions didn't make sense to her.

There is also an emotional component to communication, to which neurotypicals are attuned. They form impressions based on how a person makes them feel. A co-worker who says or does things that make them uncomfortable will be thought of unfavorably, no matter how high his intelligence or how well he performs job tasks.

NTs also adjust their behavior so that other people feel comfortable in *their* presence. Loud, angry outbursts make most people feel uncomfortable, and by and large, NTs avoid this behavior in the workplace. Repeating the same request, again and again, is annoying, so NTs usually accept "no" for an answer the first time.

Here is an example of how pragmatics, perspective taking, and context work.

You have Asperger's Syndrome and plan to ask your boss for a raise. On Monday morning, you see her in the hallway. You notice that her hair is styled differently than usual and that she is wearing high-heeled shoes instead of her usual flats. Her large gold necklace catches your attention and you wonder if she bought it as a set with the matching earrings. As you walk toward her, you repeat in your mind again and again how you will request a meeting. You silently count out the pattern in the carpet: three light blue squares followed by a large dark blue stripe. As you make your way down the hallway, you notice out of the corner of your eye that all of the offices are empty. The clock on the wall says 8:53am. You finally reach your supervisor and ask to meet. To your surprise, she replies, in an annoyed tone of voice, "Can't you *see* that this is not a good time?!"

Although you noticed many specific, physical details about the environment, your supervisor's reaction indicates that you missed something important.

Let's replay the situation, adding to what you already noticed. When you see your boss in the hallway, you also notice that she glances at her watch and takes quick steps in the direction of the conference room, indicating that she is in a hurry. You hear the sound of distant chattering while simultaneously passing empty offices. You realize that the vice presidents have assembled in the conference room and are waiting for a meeting to begin. The smell of eggs, bacon and coffee reminds you that whenever the senior management team convenes, they are served a catered breakfast. You recall that your boss spent most of the previous Thursday and Friday working on a presentation.

This time, you noticed the contextually relevant pieces of information, which suggest that your boss is running late for an important meeting. You realize that this is not a good time to approach her about a raise. By filtering out irrelevant details, such as the pattern in the rug, the exact time, and your boss's gold jewelry, you concentrate on the important clues: your supervisor's rushed appearance, the sounds coming from the conference room, and the empty offices of the vice presidents.

The basic communication principles discussed in this chapter will be further detailed in up-coming chapters of this book. They are central to your ability to understand and meet the expectations of a supervisor, interact well with co-workers, and make good social decisions. In particular, try to heighten your awareness of situational context and the people around you.

MOST COMMUNICATION IS NONVERBAL

Neurotypicals rely more on nonverbal signals to understand what someone is communicating than the words that they say.

Dr. Albert Mehrabian wrote about nonverbal communication and emotions in a book called *Silent Messages*. He discovered that 7 percent of what people communicate about their feelings and attitudes comes from their words; 38 percent comes from the way they say those words; and 55 percent comes from their facial expression (Mehrabian 1981).

When I speak to groups, I demonstrate the power of nonverbal communication by folding my arms across my chest, looking at the floor, and saying in a flat, monotone voice, "I'm very happy to be here talking to you about Asperger's Syndrome." Then, I ask whether anyone believes what I just said. Everyone says, "No." Although I *say* that I am happy to be giving the presentation, I communicate what I really feel by the *way* I say the words and my body language.

People communicate nonverbally in many ways. Body language includes facial expression, posture, gestures, proximity to others, and the orientation of one's body (whether a person is turned toward or away from someone). *Paralanguage* refers to the way that something is said: the volume and tone of voice, rate of speech, and the emphasis placed on a word or phrase (Young and Travis 2008). "You did a *great* job on that" implies work well done. "You did a great job on *that*" is a sarcastic way to indicate that expectations were not met.

Other, less obvious forms of nonverbal communication include artifacts and chronemics. "Artifacts" are items in your personal space, such as furniture, artwork, and jewelry (Young and Travis 2008). In the workplace, these items can send powerful messages. Imagine walking into a business executive's office and seeing an Angry Birds (or other video game) poster on the wall. How confident would you feel about this executive's judgment and ability to make complex decisions?

"Chronemics" refers to how the use of time communicates, "how we view others, what our culture values, and how efficient we are" (Young and Travis 2008, p.9). In our culture, habitually arriving late for appointments is interpreted as a lack of respect for the other person's time. Dominating meetings with long, detailed soliloquies about pet projects suggests lack of interest in other people's ideas.

Here is an example of how a person's body language and way of speaking communicate the real meaning of a situation, that will not be obvious based on words alone.

Tom's supervisor was not happy with Tom's performance as a customer service representative. One month earlier, Tom had disclosed having Asperger's Syndrome. At that time, I had met with Tom, his supervisor, Nancy, and the human resources manager to clarify what needed to change, and to discuss accommodations. Tom, Nancy and I were meeting again to review Tom's progress.

My first hint that Nancy was still not very happy with Tom's performance came when she entered the reception area and nodded a hello, deftly avoiding my handshake. When we reached the conference room, Tom was already seated. I listened as Nancy dutifully reviewed each item in his performance improvement plan. Her voice was tense and her eyes were fixed on the form in front of her. She gazed briefly at Tom as she delivered clipped answers to his questions, while rhythmically tapping a pen against her palm. I asked when she expected Tom to make the changes on her list. "Immediately," Nancy replied, looking me straight in the eye. I winced inside.

Nancy's refusal to shake my hand, and her silence as we walked from the reception area to the conference room, told me immediately that she did not want to have the meeting. Otherwise, she would have looked at me, smiled, shaken my hand and exchanged some pleasantries. The tension in her voice, brief glances at Tom, and continual pen tapping signaled her impatience. "She's going through the motions," I thought. If she believed that Tom could meet the performance requirements, she would have spoken in a friendly, earnest tone while maintaining eye contact. By choosing to punctuate the word "immediately" with a stare, Nancy made it very clear to me that she had run out of patience with Tom.

After the meeting, Tom and I went to the employee cafeteria to talk about what happened. "I think that went pretty well," Tom said. I told him that I didn't agree. I described to Tom my impression of the conversation, and we reviewed what he could do to try and meet Nancy's expectations. Unfortunately, my impressions were correct, and the meeting had been a formality. Tom was fired ten days later.

Nonverbal signals can help you gauge a person's confidence, enthusiasm, nervousness, excitement, boredom, and other states of mind. They enable you to deduce what someone wants you to do, such as join them in a conversation or activity, come back later, stop talking, or leave.

People also use body language to signal what *they* want to do, such as get back to their work, change topics, or end a meeting.

ⓘ *NT Tip*

When an NT is ready to end a conversation or meeting, he often speaks in the past tense: "It *was* nice to meet you;" "I'm glad we *had* the chance to get that settled;" "This *was* a good discussion."

He may also close a file folder, push his chair back slightly, glance at the computer screen (indicating thoughts about other work), fold his arms, or stand up.

There are many books that describe the meaning of body language, and computerized tests designed to measure your ability to interpret facial expressions. However, correctly interpreting nonverbal signals is often dependent on situational context.

At the urging of clients, I have taken tests where I had to look at a photograph of someone's face, and match their expression to the right emotion. My score was very low every time! There were no contextual clues to add meaning to facial expressions that sometimes were very similar. This is why I suggest that clients practice noticing and interpreting nonverbal communication by watching a movie or television program with the sound turned down. That way, they can notice the contextual clues that suggest what the characters are thinking and feeling.

In addition to observing other people's body language, you must pay attention to your own. Otherwise, *you* might be sending unintended messages. You will appear to be uninterested, bored, angry or aloof if you:

- stare at the floor or ceiling during a conversation

- slump in your chair

- fold your arms across your chest

- fiddle with a pen, rubber band or paper clip during a conversation

- speak in a monotone, or too loudly

- stare into space as you try to think of an answer to a question (instead say, "Let me think about that for a moment")

- stare, which is looking into someone's eyes for ten seconds or more

- don't smile.

With practice, most people can improve their ability to recognize and interpret nonverbal signals. If you find this to be very difficult or impossible, explain your situation using neutral language. This way, people will not take your behavior personally. You can explain: "I'm very literal, so tell me directly what I need to do;" or "Sometimes when I'm concentrating, I forget to say hello.

Please don't take it personally;" or "People tell me that I look angry when I'm lost in thought. Tell me if you notice that."

ⓘ *NT Tip*

Michelle Garcia Winner is a speech language pathologist who has developed the Social Thinking® methodology to help individuals improve their interpersonal skills. I highly recommend her book, co-authored by Pamela Crooke, *Social Thinking at Work, Why Should I Care?* (Winner and Crooke 2011).

CHAPTER 3

MAKING THE RIGHT FIRST IMPRESSION AND FITTING IN

The expression "you only get one chance to make a first impression" is true. Research has shown that most people begin forming opinions about others within the first 30 seconds of meeting. Once an opinion is formed, it is usually hard to change.

The impression you make during the first days and weeks at a new job will be lasting. In addition to being evaluated on your ability to perform tasks, you are being evaluated on whether you are able to work well with other people in the organization. All companies hire employees on a conditional basis, whether or not this is stated. This probationary status can last from two weeks to three months.

Employers hire people who they believe will "fit in" to the organization. This is an abstract concept that cannot be precisely defined. Yet it plays a large part in whether you will be successful on the job. At the most basic level, fitting in means that others in the company are comfortable working with you. The primary ways that you fit in are:

- being friendly and helpful

- arriving to work on time, appropriately dressed and groomed

- respecting the contributions and ideas of other people

- observing rules and procedures

- accepting feedback and following instructions

- handling disagreements and conflict in a mature way

- keeping emotions under control

- following the cultural norms of the organization (also known as "corporate culture").

The above topics are discussed in detail in later chapters of this book.

When you are a new employee, there are several things that you can do to make a positive first impression on your colleagues:

- *Treat the first days and weeks on the job as a time to learn* about specific job tasks, your co-workers, and how things get done at this company. Do not suggest different ways to do things until you understand how and why tasks are done in the current manner. Certain procedures probably affect other areas of the company in ways that you are not aware of.

  Ian was hired as a sales associate at a retail store. During the training period, he continually interrupted the manager to point out what he saw as inefficiencies in the customer check-out process. At first, the manager patiently explained how the system was set up so that employees in the accounting, purchasing, and other departments would get information they needed to do their jobs. Still, Ian persisted with making suggestions. He was fired after less than one week.

- *Follow instructions.* Insisting on doing things your own way will irritate your supervisor and co-workers. Especially when you are new, you should abide by the policies and procedures established at *this* company.

  Lynne was having trouble adapting to different systems and procedures in her new job. "At my last company, people appreciated it when I made suggestions," she said, "but my new supervisor gets annoyed and tells me to just do what I am told." Lynne was successful in her previous position, and didn't understand her new employer's resistance to change.

  However, Lynne didn't consider that the changes she proposed would cost the company tens of thousands of dollars, require hours of staff training, and not result in any significant increase in productivity. On closer examination, she realized that her suggestions were driven by *her* dislike of change, and her anxiety about learning a new system.

- *Stay within your assigned areas of responsibility.* It is not okay to start doing someone else's work, even if you believe that you can do it better, or to create your own project because you are bored. If you finish your assigned tasks early, ask your supervisor what you should do next.

- *Arrive on time, neatly dressed, and properly groomed.* If you look sloppy and unprofessional, people will assume that your work is sloppy and unprofessional, too. Arriving late signals poor organizational skills and lack of enthusiasm for the job. People who do not bathe often enough develop body odor, and are very unpleasant to be around. Whether you wear a uniform or clothing of your own choosing, make sure that it is clean, pressed and in compliance with the company's dress code (the employee handbook will explain the dress code). You want co-workers to focus on your abilities, not your wrinkled clothes, unusual hairstyle, or bad smell!

- *Refrain from making negative comments* about current or previous supervisors, co-workers or employers. Your new colleagues want to work with people who are pleasant and enthusiastic. They avoid people who are perceived as chronic complainers. Do not launch into long stories about the idiots you used to work with, what a loser your boss was, or how crappy this company's benefits are compared to what you had with a previous employer.

   This does not mean that you can never vent frustrations on the job. As long as it is not taken to extremes, commiserating with your colleagues about various difficulties or disappointments can reduce stress levels and build strong relationships. However, until you know who you can trust to keep this type of communication private, make only positive comments at work.

- *Wait until people finish speaking before you begin talking.* Interrupting people makes them think that you are not listening or not interested in what they have to say. One man, who works from a home office, keeps his phone on "mute" during meetings as a reminder to let people finish speaking before he makes a comment. If you are concerned that you will forget your point if you don't speak up right away, write it down. Some people carry a small notepad for this purpose.

   If you have trouble knowing when someone else has finished speaking, practice the three-second pause. When you *think* that someone is done, silently count to three. If they don't say more, they have probably finished. You can practice this by listening to audio recordings of people speaking, or watching television talk shows.

   You can also ask a co-worker who you trust to give you subtle signals when you interrupt. You can arrange this by saying, "I want to break my habit of interrupting. Would you [cough, clear your throat, tap your ear] to let me know when I do it?"

If interrupting is a serious problem, you will know when people frequently tell you to stop doing it. Confront it in a direct way. Notice when you interrupt. Is it during meetings, or one-on-one conversations with certain people? Seek help from a professional to break this habit.

- *Show people that you are listening.* If you look away while someone is speaking, or stare at them with a blank facial expression, they will think that you are bored or not paying attention. If you are very uncomfortable making eye contact, or find it hard to simultaneously look at someone and listen to what he says, approximate eye contact by glancing at the space between a person's eyebrows. Nodding your head periodically indicates that you are listening (not that you agree with what is said). Occasional, brief comments, such as "I see" or "I understand," also communicate that the speaker has your attention.

Adam's supervisor told him that he needed to pay attention during staff meetings. This confused Adam, who said that he listened intently to everything that was said. During the meetings, Adam stared at his notepad. "Looking at a person when they are speaking communicates that you are listening," I explained. Adam began doing this, and a few weeks later, his supervisor praised him for being more involved in the meetings!

HOW TO INTRODUCE YOURSELF TO CO-WORKERS

Expect to be introduced to co-workers during the first few days at a new job. Unless the company is very small, you will not meet every employee. Typically, you will be introduced to other members of your department or work group, and individuals from other areas of the company with whom you will interact on a regular basis. These introductions can be made by your supervisor, a peer in your department, or a human resources manager.

Your goal is to appear enthusiastic and friendly. The best way to do this is to smile. I consider this to be a basic job skill. If you meet someone with an expressionless stare, you will appear to be bored, uninterested, or even hostile.

If you often forget to smile, make it a priority to practice this skill until it becomes automatic. Begin by smiling in front of a mirror so that you can find the point where you look friendly and relaxed. Pay attention to how your mouth feels and looks. If possible, ask family members to remind you to smile when you see them. Smiling actually changes the sound of your voice. It also can improve your mood if you are upset or down. Salespeople are taught to smile when they pick up the telephone because it makes them sound friendlier and more enthusiastic.

Smiling puts people at ease, and important to do whenever you are saying hello or goodbye.

The person escorting you will announce your name and position to the other employees you meet: "Tom, this is Sara Adams, our new research associate. Sara, this is Tom Jones, our marketing director." Respond by looking the individual in the eye, smiling, and extending your right hand. When you shake hands, the area between your thumb and forefinger should be nestled against the same area on the other person's right hand. Squeeze their hand firmly and say your greeting. It will help you remember the person if you use his first name in your greeting: "Hi, Tom, it's nice to meet you!" or "Hello, Tom, I'm looking forward to working with you." Two to three shakes are enough.

These introductions are for the purpose of showing you around the workplace and acquainting you with some colleagues. You are not expected to remember the name of every person you meet. If someone asks you a question, such as where you previously worked, answer briefly: "For the past two years, I worked in the research group at ACME Corporation."

USING SMALL TALK TO BUILD RELATIONSHIPS

"I didn't know that just saying, 'Hi, how are you?' is a key to opening relationships, not a question that needs answering." (Food Service Worker and Educator, age 56)

My coaching clients have some pretty definite opinions about small talk. I have heard it described as: a waste of time; a nonsensical NT ritual; stupid; boring; and "something that I can't do." Some declare that they have no interest in even trying to learn this skill.

However, small talk is the first step in establishing relationships with your colleagues. Neurotypicals place a high value on workplace relationships. I have seen numerous surveys where people rate a good relationship with their supervisor, and liking their co-workers, as major factors in their job satisfaction.

Trading a few friendly remarks about the weather or the traffic with fellow employees you see in the lunch room, or in the elevator, sends the message that you consider yourself part of the group. Participating in chatter with the people you work with frequently is the basis for building camaraderie and trust. People want to work with colleagues who they like and who are dependable. They are usually much more forgiving of errors and eccentricities if they perceive you as cooperative and friendly.

You do not need to actually *like* someone to act friendly toward them at work. These are things that you can do to make yourself appear friendly:

- Greet co-workers in the morning by saying, "Good morning," or asking, "Hi, how are you?"

- Smile when you greet people or pass them in the hallway.

- Accept an invitation to join your colleagues for lunch, as this is a gesture of friendliness.

- Attend office holiday parties and talk to people while you are there, even if you only converse with people in your department. Act like you are having a good time, even if you are not.

- Show an interest in others, both in the projects they are working on and how they are personally.

  ### ⓘ *NT Tip*
  Be gracious when someone gives you a compliment by smiling and saying thank you. It is considered rude to reject the compliment by explaining why you don't deserve it: "The work was easy and I had no trouble with it;" or by questioning the person's taste: "What do you find attractive about this old watch?"

HOW TO MAKE A REASONABLE AMOUNT OF SMALL TALK

Small talk is a brief, back-and-forth exchange of questions and comments about neutral topics, such as the weather, sports, traffic, a national news item, or someone's plans for the weekend. The purpose of small talk is to establish and maintain friendly relationships. It is not for exchanging important information. People typically engage in small talk for five minutes or less.

You do not need to follow sports, or watch popular programs on television, to find neutral topics for small talk. Staying reasonably up to date on local and national news is a way to find topics that other people will know about. Many local news stations have websites that summarize noteworthy events. It only takes a few minutes each day to read some of the featured stories. If someone brings up a topic that you are not familiar with, you can join the discussion by making a comment or asking a question about it: "Sounds like that was an exciting baseball game" or "I didn't hear about the accident on the highway. What happened?"

Avoid topics that polarize people, such as politics, religion, or race; or those that make people uncomfortable, such as sex and gossip about other employees. Personal observations about a person's weight, clothing, hair style and mannerisms should also be avoided.

Despite being a talented software developer, Susan has been fired from numerous jobs. "I've been lambasted for being 'rude,' 'nasty,' and 'offensive' for saying things that I thought were benign or supportive," she complained. One day, she was sharing lunch with a co-worker who was lamenting about numerous failed weight loss attempts. Intending to be sympathetic, Susan said, "I can see that the diets aren't working because you're still fat." The co-worker complained to Susan's supervisor.

The key is to keep the conversation going for at least two or three turns. If you respond to someone's comment or question with a one-word answer, or by saying, "I don't know," it will end the conversation. You are in the break room and someone asks whether you saw a particular television program. You say, "No." The message you have sent is that you do not want to interact with the individual.

However, if you reply with a comment or question, you are expressing interest in continuing the interaction:

You reply, "I haven't seen that program, what is it about?"

The other person says, "It's a drama about physicians who work in the emergency room. They deal with all kinds of accidents and illnesses."

You continue to show your interest by commenting, "That sounds like an interesting show. When is it on?"

Your co-worker replies, "Tuesdays at 10:00. When I was younger, I wanted to be a doctor."

Now, you have received some interesting information about your co-worker, that could lead to a more in-depth discussion. You might continue, "How come you didn't pursue medicine?"

Here is another example of how chatting about something inconsequential can be the start of a more substantial relationship:

Jim sees you in the break room and asks, "Did you get caught in that traffic jam on Route 66?"

Instead of saying "No" and ending the exchange, you say, "No, I live in Smithtown so I don't take the highway to get here."

"I used to drive through Smithtown when I worked at ACME Widgetworks," Jim says.

You respond, "I worked at ACME six years ago, in the research and development group."

Jim replies, "I was in research and development, too. We should get together for lunch this week."

Do you see how small talk can lead to a new contact in your network, a buddy at work, or even a personal friendship?

Notice how each individual in the examples asked a question or made a comment about the same topic. Small talk, like longer conversations, is a reciprocal exchange. Simply asking someone a series of unrelated questions, without sharing your thoughts or experiences, makes it seem that you are grilling the other person for information. That is not establishing a relationship.

Making small talk is an important business skill to learn. Even though it may feel very uncomfortable to you at first, it will get easier with practice. Experiment outside of the workplace by striking up brief exchanges with store clerks, bank tellers, or the mailman.

⊙ *NT Tip*
> A highly recommended resource for learning conversational skills is *How to Start a Conversation and Make Friends* by Don Gabor (1983).

ANATOMY OF A WELCOME LUNCH

It had taken a whopping 43 interviews, but Andy had finally managed to land his first job after getting his degree in accounting. He called out a cheery hello as he strode into my office, without as much as a nod in my direction. Spying a bowl of M&Ms on the credenza, he helped himself to a generous handful and settled into a chair to start the coaching session.

The topic was how to act at a welcome lunch taking place on Andy's first day. It would include seven of Andy's fellow new hires, Andy's supervisor, and the head of the department. Despite his extroversion and desire to fit in, social communication didn't come easily to Andy. "I don't want to do anything dumb on my first day!" he said.

The first order of business was to clarify the purpose of the lunch. When I explained that the conversation would not focus on accounting, Andy raised his eyebrows.

"The lunch is a chance for people to get to know each other," I said.

"You mean schmoozing!" Andy said, laughing.

We discussed that he did not have to order salad (the texture of lettuce bothered him), and that it would be wise to avoid an entrée that was messy to eat, like spaghetti. The intricacies of conversation were a bit tougher. Andy's special interest was numbers. During stressful events, such as socializing, he looked for opportunities to turn conversations toward the merits of various tax deductions, the toughest questions on the Certified Public Accountant exam, and his projected 401(k) savings at retirement. Andy also had a hard time participating in conversations if he was not personally interested in the topic.

We established that Andy would be conversing primarily with the people sitting to his immediate left and right, and directly in front of him at the table. We reviewed how to listen to the conversations going on around him, and join one by asking a question or making a comment. Then I threw him a proverbial curve ball.

"What if none of the conversations is interesting," I asked, "What would you do then?"

Andy thought for a moment and replied, "Put my hands over my ears and stare at the wall."

When he thought about it, Andy realized that this would communicate to his co-workers that he did not want to be part of their group. People would find his behavior to be very odd, and this would create a negative impression of Andy. We discussed that he would need to pretend to be interested, and participate with questions and comments, in order to be perceived in a positive way.

In many organizations, a new employee is invited to lunch on his first day. This could be a formal event, arranged by a supervisor for every member of a department. Or, it could be a simple invitation to join a group of co-workers in the lunch room. As Andy learned, the real purpose of the lunch is for you and your new colleagues to get to know one another, and to make you feel welcome. While some business may be discussed, you should expect to share personal information. For example, you might be asked about how you got into the field or profession; where you worked previously; and why you left your last job. More personal questions could be what town you live in; whether you are married or have children; where you grew up; or about your hobbies.

Your responses should be positive. If you had a bad experience at a previous job, do not share the details. Discuss it in a neutral way: "I learned a lot at TriMerica, but it was time for a bigger challenge" or "I especially enjoy launching new products, which is why this job was so appealing."

Similarly, your response to personal inquiries should be upbeat and general. This is a business activity, even though people may discuss aspects of their personal lives. It is not appropriate to share details about your messy divorce, your spouse's health crisis, or that you now live in an apartment because your home was foreclosed.

Show an interest in learning about your colleagues, too. You might ask: "My husband and I have been married for 11 years; how about you?" or "How did you get into engineering?" or "What do you like most about working here?" or "What kind of projects do you handle?"

You may or may not be expected to pay for your lunch. Observe what happens when the check arrives. If it is a formal event, and your supervisor takes the check, thank him for the lunch. If you see that people are reaching for their wallets, do the same. If each individual is paying, it is expected that the check will be evenly divided among them. It is bad form to add up the cost of your meal, calculate a tip, and pay the exact amount. If your co-workers say that they are paying for your lunch as a welcoming gesture, accept their generosity and say thank you.

ⓘ NT Tip

If it is your first day and you brought your lunch to work, do not refuse an invitation to join your co-workers at a restaurant. This would make food seem more important than getting to know the people you will be working with. You can save your lunch for the next day.

Your efforts to be interested in your co-workers should not end after a welcome lunch or brief introduction. Select one or two individuals you interact with regularly, whom you would like to know better. Be alert for opportunities to find out more about them during a break, before a meeting starts, or when you are leaving work to go home.

Building relationships takes time and consistent effort. Act in ways that signal your willingness to connect. Sam realized that sitting at his cubicle with headphones on from 9:00am to 5:00pm sent a message to colleagues to stay away. Bill forced himself to leave his office door open for several hours a day, so that he would be perceived as accessible by his colleagues.

You do not need to interact with other people all day, or become a world-class communicator, in order to fit in. The key is to do enough to establish yourself as open, friendly and trustworthy. If you make a sincere effort to cultivate good working relationships with others, people will probably sense that, and accept some awkwardness or social gaffes.

WHY YOU NEED A WORK BUDDY

"Instead of trying to fit in with numerous people at once, find one who fits in well with the others and allow the person to instruct you as you go along. I have a co-worker who jokingly states that he will help 'take the ass out of Asperger's.'" (Inventory Control Specialist, age 32)

Many years ago, I read that someone had figured out 200 different ways to wash dishes. This underscored that there are many different methods for achieving the same result.

This is also true in the workplace. Every organization has unique systems and processes. Even if you have the same job at a new company, there will be differences in procedures, policies, and equipment. The reporting structures may be different. Certainly the people will be, and they will have different expectations, preferences, and communication styles. The company culture might also be a departure from your previous experience (see the section in Chapter 4, "A Primer on Office Politics," for more about corporate culture).

The unique way that "things get done around here" can only be learned on the job, and from your co-workers. This is why I believe that one of the most important employment success strategies you can implement is to find a "work buddy."

A work buddy is a colleague, preferably a peer or someone in your department. This should not be your supervisor or a human resources representative. This is someone who can help you to understand and learn the many specific details about how to do your job and interact with others in the company. Sometimes, this is a formally established partnership with a designated mentor or trainer. More often, a work buddy is someone who you like and trust.

There are many benefits of having a work buddy. He can translate unspoken workplace rules for you: what is a priority, how your supervisor prefers to get information, whom you can trust and whom you should avoid. He can explain office politics—who in the organization really has power, how decisions get made, what qualities are valued, and how various departments or divisions interact.

Your buddy can also provide concrete ideas about how to work efficiently. Richard was having a difficult time managing his job after his company reduced staffing levels. In the past, he was able to compensate for his slower, more methodical work style by putting in a few extra hours each week. Recently, he was working eleven- and twelve-hour days. "I don't know how much longer I can handle the stress," he said, "my boss just tells me that I need to be more efficient."

Richard's attempts at increased efficiency weren't working. Somehow, he managed to choose the wrong shortcuts. He ignored a deadline on a project that was critical. He decided to skip a meeting called by the senior vice president, that everyone else attended. He didn't respond to urgent emails in a timely fashion. Richard sought out a peer who was able to explain the true priorities, what tasks could wait, and which meetings were important to attend.

Paul was overwhelmed by the weekly volume of patients that he had to manage in his job as a physician's assistant. He couldn't determine whether he was processing paperwork too slowly or simply had too many patients to see. Paul asked his buddy, a fellow physician's assistant, to review his case-management methods. The co-worker showed Paul shortcuts that saved four hours of administrative time per week.

Dan's buddy was able to give him excellent advice about how to handle various conflicts and frustrations. Once, he stopped Dan from sending an angry email to the director of the IT department. "He talked me out of something that could really have damaged my reputation, or gotten me fired," Dan said.

We all need a reality check from time to time, and this is another way that your work buddy can be of great value. This person can provide feedback about things such as: Is my supervisor critical of just my work, or of everyone else's, too? Are other people confused by the new system, or it is just me? Is everyone overwhelmed or am I the only one who can't keep up? Do other departments have conflicts with the head of marketing or is it only my group? Was that comment a joke or a put-down?

Choose your work buddy with care. This person needs to be someone whom you explicitly trust, especially if you decide to tell him about your Asperger's Syndrome. Signs that a co-worker will make a good work buddy include the following:

- having patience when answering your questions: they don't say, "I'm surprised you don't know that;" or "It's obvious;" or "Weren't you paying attention?"

- volunteering information that is important for you to know, such as: things that annoy your supervisor, who is trustworthy, or who to go to with questions

- introducing you to other people in the company

- making sure that you are invited to lunches with your department or team members, or to social events outside the office.

Once you have identified a colleague with these characteristics, it is not necessary to ask that he or she become your work buddy. This will happen naturally over time. Be careful not to overwhelm this person with too many questions and requests for advice. Build the relationship through interaction and becoming friendly.

Express gratitude for the assistance you receive: "Thanks, Bill, for filling me in on the situation with Steve." Be alert for ways to reciprocate, such as offering to pitch in if your buddy has a lot of work, bringing him a cup of coffee, or taking him to lunch. You do not need to "keep score," that is, do something for the person every time he does something for you. If you are uncertain of appropriate ways to show appreciation, talk the situation over with someone outside of work.

ASKING FOR HELP IS A GOOD THING; *BEING* TOO HELPFUL IS NOT

The one characteristic of Asperger's Syndrome that I have seen in every single client is a reluctance to ask for help. Ironically, these same individuals are usually very willing and generous with the assistance they offer to others.

Alex presumed that since he had been hired, his employer expected him to know everything about the job, on the first day. He also admitted a tendency to "reinvent the wheel," ignoring established systems and creating his own procedures for completing tasks. He noticed that his way was almost always inefficient and very time consuming.

Sarah was afraid of appearing "dumb" and would tell people that she understood things, when she really didn't. Because of this, she made many errors in her work and eventually lost her job. Ben has frequently been criticized for misinterpreting situations. Now, he is ashamed to ask for help. "I am tired of being accused of not paying attention," he sighed.

Josh didn't know who or how to ask for assistance. He feared that asking the wrong question would result in being yelled at, or losing his job. He spent many hours trying to figure things out on his own, and was often behind in his assignments.

It is normal and expected that employees will ask for help when needed. However, it is also possible to ask *too* many questions. This will annoy your supervisor and co-workers, and raise questions about your competence. Anxiety drives some people to ask questions that they already know how to answer. The queries can serve as a compulsive way of double checking their work, or a means of receiving validation that they are doing a good job. Trying to do something *exactly* right can also prompt unnecessary questions.

If you are new on the job, or are being trained on a new procedure or system, it is expected that you will have questions. Even if you had a similar position in the past, a new company will have different people, procedures and policies. This is why many organizations have formal training periods, which can last from a few days to several weeks. An experienced member of the department may be assigned to show a newcomer what needs to be done and how to do it.

Asking when you don't understand is the smart thing to do. Otherwise, you could waste a lot of time on work that will have to be redone. No matter how long you have been with a company, asking colleagues for suggestions or advice when you face a new situation will enable you to find better solutions in less time. Even top executives are encouraged to "know what they don't know," and surround themselves with people who have the missing skills, expertise or experience.

Determine to whom you should direct your requests for assistance. In jobs that are process oriented (data entry, accounts receivable, retail sales) this might clearly be your direct supervisor or a peer. If you are in a manager-level position or higher, the correct "who" depends on the nature of the inquiry. The expectation usually is that you will find answers to common, procedural items on your own or through a co-worker who is at your level. Matters that have the potential to significantly impact sales, profits, expenses, critical deadlines, or the work of people inside and outside of your department should involve your supervisor. If you are completely confused about where to go for an answer, ask a peer: "Who should I ask about X?"

Keep notes about who to contact for specific questions or problems, so that you do not have to ask this again and again. Co-workers will be irritated if they believe that you are not paying attention.

Asking too many questions may be a sign that you do not understand a fundamental part of an assignment or task. Rather than continually interrupting your colleagues, write down everything that is unclear. Arrange a meeting with your supervisor, a colleague or your work buddy to review the items on your list. If you need additional training, more practice or written instructions, say so.

If colleagues consistently resist answering your questions, this could indicate a bigger problem. If you are told, "The answer is in your training manual" or "You should know how to answer that," it means that you are expected to try to find the answer on your own. If you are told, "We discussed this last week (or several times)," you need to start taking notes, or listen more carefully in the future. "You should know that by now" may signal the need for additional training, is a sign that people are annoyed with you, or means that you are in the wrong job.

Neurotypicals may be surprised when you ask about things that are very obvious to them. They may make remarks such as: "That's obvious;" or "Common sense should tell you;" or a sarcastic, "What do you *think* the answer is?!" Refuse to be intimidated by these kinds of responses. Do not become angry, either. Handle the situation in a way that gets your question answered.

One effective technique is to say, in a sincere voice, "Actually, it is not obvious to me. Would you explain what I need to do?" or "I guess I don't have common sense. Tell me what I am missing." You can also try a bit of self-deprecating humor: "I can be rather clueless sometimes; please spell out what you need very precisely for me." Use this kind of humor sparingly, or it will appear that you lack self-confidence.

Use caution and discretion if you have questions concerning interpersonal communication and relationships. It is inappropriate to ask your supervisor how to make small talk, whether you make enough eye contact, or why your peers don't invite you to lunch. These topics are considered to be personal. Questions like these are best addressed by someone outside of the office, such as a coach, psychotherapist or family member. If you are confused about office politics, or the personality styles, preferences and expectations of others, ask your work buddy for guidance.

Clearly, asking for help when you need it is the smart thing to do. But what if you want to offer help and advice to others? Have you ever had the experience of trying to be supportive only to have people accuse you of being selfish or rude?

John was thrilled to get hired as a sales associate for a major retail chain. During his first week assisting customers on the sales floor, he received several compliments from his supervisor. By week two, things had begun to go downhill. John noticed what seemed to be glaring inefficiencies in the sales system, and began challenging his boss and the other associates about the procedures. "I thought they would be glad to know about a better way to do things," he said.

Nearly a month into the job, John was fired. One reason for his termination: refusal to follow company procedures. At our first coaching session, John slumped in his chair. "I was only trying to help and I got fired," he said.

Lisa was shocked to learn at her performance review that colleagues complained that she was critical, judgmental and a "nitpicker." At issue was her habit of correcting people when they made grammatical and pronunciation mistakes, or deviated from a standard procedure. "I thought people want to know when they've done something wrong," she said.

Both John and Lisa thought that they were making positive contributions. What happened?

In John's case, he didn't think about the big picture. Although his suggestions might have made *his* job more efficient, implementing his ideas would mean major changes to the existing systems. John suggested changes without fully understanding why certain procedures were currently in place. Additionally, he had gone outside of his assigned job responsibilities in trying to redesign the sales processes.

Lisa's mistake concerned situational context. When she was doing her copy editing, it was appropriate that she correct grammatical errors. However, within the context of staff meetings, correcting others was unwelcome and perceived as arrogant.

A general rule for offering help is this: be sure that the other person wants it. Unsolicited advice and error correction are usually unwelcome. The exceptions are situations where your comments will spare someone embarrassment: "There is mayonnaise on your chin;" or prevent an accident or serious error: "You'll be cut if you hold the blade that way."

ⓘ *NT Tip*
It is considered rude to eavesdrop on conversations, and especially rude to eavesdrop and then point out someone's error!

Be certain that your helpfulness is not violating any company policies or rules. Brendan was reprimanded for accepting returns of video games that had been opened. The store policy was to make refunds only on products in unopened packages. Although he wanted to help the customers, his first responsibility was to follow company guidelines.

HOW TO BE A TEAM PLAYER

"Talk less, listen and think about what others are saying." (IP Project Manager, age 61)

The ability to work effectively with others is a necessary skill. But what exactly makes someone a good team player?

Being a "team player" means working collaboratively with other people to reach a common goal. A team can be comprised of people in your department, individuals from different parts of the company who are collaborating on a project (this is sometimes referred to as a cross-functional team), or the members of a committee.

Each team member needs to understand how their expertise and skills contribute to the project's success. As in any group, different people will have different needs, values, personality styles and personal objectives. At times, these differences result in team conflicts.

A stated team goal, such as "create a top-quality widget," carries with it all of the unstated ambitions of the people involved. The vice president of manufacturing might see the objective as, "Create a top-quality widget…but keep production costs low." The director of marketing thinks, "Create a top-quality widget…that will be ready in time for our fall sales campaign." The vice president of sales hears, "Create a top-quality widget…that has features that our customers can't resist, so that my sales force can sell a lot of them." If the concerns and priorities of team members are too diverse or clash, it will be very difficult for the group to function cohesively, reach consensus and make decisions.

An essential aspect of teamwork is listening to and respecting the ideas of others, whether you agree with them or not! Pay attention when other people are speaking so that you can understand their problems and point of view. This information will give you a sense of the big picture and will assist you in presenting your ideas in a way that addresses the concerns of others in the group. Do not interrupt others to interject your ideas, even if you believe that what the other person is saying is wrong. You will be perceived as condescending and arrogant if you make negative comments or correct people's minor mistakes.

Brian readily admitted his contempt for what he called the "shallow" corporate expressions used by his colleagues. It wasn't until his performance review that he realized the impact of his sarcastic comments on his co-workers. "People don't think that you want to be part of the team," the supervisor said. Brian decided to make positive statements instead. Now if someone mentions "creating synergies," he responds with, "Here's how I think we can get the most out of our combined efforts."

Nancy's command of her employer's complex internal processes was lauded throughout her division. Yet her performance reviews were mediocre because she earned a reputation as difficult to work with and a poor team player. Nancy frequently interrupted people with comments like "That won't work" or "We've tried that before."

"But I *know* their ideas won't work," Nancy protested during one of our coaching sessions. "Why should I waste time letting people go on and on?"

"When you interrupt," I explained, "you are communicating that you don't respect other people's ideas, or think that they don't have anything important to contribute."

Nancy later found out that some of her co-workers interpreted her remarks to mean that she thought they were stupid.

Nancy agreed to experiment with not interrupting for the next week. This was especially difficult when she was listening to the junior members of the department. At first, Nancy noticed her rising feelings of impatience as they proposed solutions that she knew would not work. By the third day, she realized that listening enabled her to identify the areas where these employees needed additional training.

Clear communication is particularly important when you work on a team. Think what would happen on a baseball diamond or a football field, if the players had no idea what their teammates were doing. The same principle applies at work. It is a mistake to assume that other people see a situation the same way that you do, or that they will draw the same conclusions. Pete was assigned to an emergency project and presumed that his co-workers would know that his regular work would be late. His co-workers, however, assumed that everything was on schedule because Pete didn't tell them there would be delays! At his performance review, Pete was described as a poor team player.

Team interaction goes two ways. In addition to keeping colleagues informed about your work, you should make an effort to find out what they are working on as well. This demonstrates a team orientation, and will help you understand how your work fits into the whole. I have had multiple clients tell me that once they stopped tuning out at meetings, they were amazed to learn the ways that their co-workers' projects impacted their own.

Finally, good team players express enthusiasm, even if they don't always feel it. This does not mean acting in a hyper-animated way, or making gushing remarks. You can express enthusiasm by asking questions, making supportive comments, sharing helpful ideas, and listening intently when people speak.

Company culture dictates standards of teamwork. Observe how, when and where your colleagues interact. Do they socialize for a few minutes before starting meetings or do people enter the conference room and get down to business right away? Do most people in your work group eat lunch at their desks or do they eat together in the lunch room? Do they get together after work? As much as possible, match your level of social interaction with that of your teammates.

ⓘ *NT Tip*

There are times when it is acceptable and desirable to disagree with colleagues. State your opinion in neutral terms, such as "I see the situation differently" or "Here's how I look at it." Judgmental phrases like "That's dumb" or "Anyone can see that" make people defensive and less inclined to listen to your point of view.

MEETING EMPLOYER EXPECTATIONS

"Find a way to prioritize based on what your employer needs from you, not what you think is important." (Industrial Hygienist, age 50)

Obviously, meeting the expectations of your employer is crucial if you want to keep your job. Yet, understanding exactly what the expectations are is not always straightforward. Neurotypicals will not explicitly spell out tasks that they consider to be obvious. There is an assumption that an employee will deduce and understand certain tasks, based on past experience or by observing co-workers.

Melissa's supervisor complained that she was taking too long to clear tables at the restaurant where she worked. Instead of placing all of the dirty dishes into a bin and making one trip to the kitchen, as her co-workers did, Melissa removed dirty items by category: one trip for silverware, another for glassware, a third trip to wipe down the table. She didn't understand why the more efficient process of making one trip hadn't been explained to her.

Employer expectations fall into distinct categories. There is basic employment readiness, which means arriving on time, rested, and ready to work; observing the rules regarding breaks and lunch; dressing appropriately; and following instructions. Alex's supervisor expressed surprise that Alex literally ran out of the building at the end of the day. "He said this is unprofessional," Alex explained, "But I don't want to miss my train."

The second category concerns performance. This involves completing tasks correctly and on time, and meeting productivity requirements (the quantity of work to be finished within a certain time period).

Working with other people, inside and outside of the company, is the third category. This includes the so-called people skills, such as listening to others, accepting feedback, communicating clearly, and collaborating.

Some of my clients have trouble meeting expectations because they do not fully listen to instructions. True listening involves more than hearing the words that someone says, as we have been discussing throughout this book. Situational context, tone and volume of voice, facial expression and body language all play a role in defining the *meaning* of a person's words.

Rich was so anxious about doing a good job, that he would "guess and go." When his supervisor explained a task, he would focus on one or two words, and start working without fully understanding what was required. If he received verbal instructions, he would forget some of the steps.

Bill's resistance to change made it hard for him to be productive. It upset him that his new company used an unfamiliar software program. Bill thought that the product he used previously was better. Rather than focus on learning how to use the new software, Bill spent the equivalent of several work days comparing and contrasting the two products, speaking with vendors, and composing a report explaining why the company should switch. Bill quickly fell behind on his first assignment. After learning that the company would not purchase new software, Bill continued to extol the merits of his preferred product. Shortly before his probationary period was up, Bill was let go.

Curtis described how he "lost his way" within his first month as an analyst. He could perform various calculations accurately, but became mired in details and drifted off on tangents. He spent excessive amounts of time performing what-if scenarios that had no relevance to his projects. At staff meetings, Curtis was unable to draw conclusions from the data and answer basic business questions.

His boss thought that Curtis wasn't paying attention or putting enough effort into his work. The real problem was that Curtis did not understand the purpose of his job. As a result, it was hard to know which details were important, how much needed to be done, and when a task was complete.

Trouble seeing the big picture affected Meghan's ability to learn how to enter information into a database. In the past, she has lost jobs because she couldn't learn processes quickly enough. I listened as she described her confusion. Then I said, "The purpose of the database is to organize information about the company's customers. Information, such as their names, addresses, and the products they have purchased, can be used in various ways. For example, the marketing department might select customers who bought a particular product, and offer them a related item."

"Ohhhh," Meghan said. "Why didn't anyone tell me that?"

Previously, databases had appeared to Meghan as a collection of random, unconnected fields to fill in. At each job, slight variations in a particular software program completely confused Meghan. She started from scratch each time, trying to remember what information needed to be entered, and where.

However, once she understood the purpose of the database (the big picture), Meghan saw the flow of information, and how similar one database software program was to another. Rather than try to memorize the placement of random bits of information, Meghan was now able to think in terms of basic customer information: name, address, telephone, email, products purchased, cost, and so on.

Understanding the purpose of a task, and how it fits into the company's business, helps you know what you need to do.

I have coached individuals who were stunned to receive poor performance reviews, or lose jobs. "I thought everything was fine," they exclaim. "Why wasn't I told that there was a problem with my work?" It turns out that they *were* being told of performance shortfalls, but in ways that they didn't understand.

Seth was having problems adapting to a new supervisor and expanded job duties. His primary responsibility was to edit a professional journal in the life sciences industry. Recently, he was given additional production tasks, such as formatting articles. Seth was finding it hard to keep up.

He was told that he had two months to correct his performance problems or be fired. His supervisor, Marcia, didn't think that Seth was making the needed changes. "She says that I'm not trying, because I am not following her suggestions to use checklists, prepare for meetings, and try to find answers to questions on my own," Seth sighed.

Probing Seth for more details, he explained how stressful it was when Marcia fired one question after another at him about the status of his projects. "The stress makes my brain shut down," he said. In response, Seth spent more and more of his time editing, an activity that he was good at and enjoyed. The production tasks were left undone, and the publication slipped farther and farther behind schedule.

Seth did not proactively address his supervisor's concerns. He dismissed her suggestions as useless, not realizing that she was telling him very directly what he needed to change. His anxiety about the new responsibilities prompted Seth to focus on familiar activities. He knew that he was neglecting critical aspects of his job, but felt paralyzed about taking action.

If you, like Seth, are experiencing ongoing problems meeting expectations, a more proactive approach is in order. This is especially true if you are responsible for managing projects or people, or have a professional position.

Ignoring problems, or passively waiting for your supervisor to suggest solutions, sends the message that you are not motivated to change.

Here is a three-step technique for better problem-solving:

1. Define the specific problem that you need to address.

2. Describe the *end result* that you want.

3. Brainstorm possible solutions and predict their likely outcomes.

If necessary, enlist the help of a family member, friend, or a professional.

When Seth tried this technique, he was surprised at how many solutions he found. He defined one problem as: *Marcia says that I ask her too many detailed questions about the production process. She expects that I will find the answers to 80 percent of these questions on my own.*

Seth defined the result that he wanted: *I want Marcia to see that I am resourceful, can work independently, and that I am listening to her and making changes.*

Next he brainstormed possible solutions and predicted what the likely outcomes would be:

*   Solution 1: *Keep asking Marcia questions; she is my boss and it is her job to answer them. Likely outcome: Marcia will continue to be frustrated with me and think that I cannot do the job.*

*   Solution 2: *Ask one of the other editors, who has production experience, for suggestions on how to organize the process. Take detailed notes. Likely outcome: This will probably answer most of my questions, and I will have written instructions to use.*

*   Solution 3: *Research books and courses on magazine production. Ask our printer and graphic designer for recommendations. Likely outcome: A better understanding of the entire process.*

Seth implemented solution two, and within two weeks, the magazine was back on schedule. Marcia noticed the improvement.

At first, Seth found the process of brainstorming solutions and predicting outcomes to be time consuming. I encouraged him to stick with it. Some of the solutions he identified served as templates that could be applied to similar situations. The more he practiced, the easier the problem-solving process became.

You can also use this exercise to work on interpersonal communication skills. Tina has been fired from two jobs because her colleagues considered her to be rude and difficult to work with. It had never occurred to Tina that she could change the way that other people perceive her. She began by defining the specific problem: *People think that I am rude because I snap at them and yell when I am stressed.* Next, she described her desired result: *I want people to perceive me as friendly and cooperative.*

Together, we brainstormed several possible solutions, and their likely outcomes:

- Solution 1: *Stop talking to people altogether. Likely outcome: I will be seen as even more unfriendly; this solution is unrealistic because I have to talk to people to get my work done.*

- Solution 2: *Join co-workers for lunch once per week. Likely outcome: People will see that I am making an effort; it might be awkward because I am not sure of what to say.*

- Solution 3: *Find ways to manage stress. Likely outcome: If I am calm and more relaxed, I won't yell.*

- Solution 4: *Observe how my peers interact and emulate behaviors that demonstrate friendliness. Likely outcome: People will like me better and want to work with me.*

Although Tina liked the idea of joining her co-workers for lunch, she was very anxious about how to act. It was too big a step at that time. Tina decided to implement solutions three and four, coming up with specific, small actions for each.

STRATEGIES FOR CLARIFYING EXPECTATIONS

- *Know the purpose of what you are doing.* How does your task or project contribute to the goals of your department and/or the company? Who will utilize what you produce? For what purpose? What is most important to the end user? If you cannot answer these questions, you need to discover the big picture. Try a general inquiry to a colleague or your supervisor: "I want to be sure that I understand how everything fits together. Can you walk me through how the analyses will be used?" If you know or suspect that you are confused about something that is obvious to others, use a more direct approach: "I'm so detail oriented that I sometimes lose track of the big picture. What are the priorities?"

- *Ask to see a sample* if you are unsure of what a finished product should look like. You may also be able to find examples by searching the internet. Alternately, you can submit an outline, so that you can receive feedback before you put too much time into a project.

- *Ask for assistance* if you do not know how to get started on a task or assignment: "Where's the best place to start?" or "How do you recommend that I get started?"

- *Request written instructions, or time to take notes,* when you are learning a new process. If a co-worker becomes impatient, say: "If I don't write this down, I won't remember all of the steps. Writing it down means that we only need to review it once."

- *Summarize your understanding of an assignment*: "You want me to update the ledger first, and then start processing the checks." Summarize using your own words. If you repeat what the other person said verbatim, it will look like you are not paying attention.

- *Ask your supervisor his preference* for how often he wants updates, how you should handle questions, and what decisions you can make independently.

- *Observe your peers to discover unspoken expectations.* Anna noticed that when there were few customers in the retail store, her fellow sales associates would take unsold clothing from the dressing rooms, and return it to racks on the sales floor.

- *Ask for feedback about your performance at regular intervals.* The frequency depends on your job and length of employment. If you are newly hired, requesting feedback from your supervisor after two weeks is appropriate. If you are a manager, ask for a one-month review. Don't ask too often, or you will appear insecure.

  Frame your request in a positive manner: "I want to be sure that I'm meeting your expectations. Can we set up a meeting next week to discuss my performance?" If the first session goes well, it may not be necessary to schedule another meeting until your regular performance review. If your supervisor recommends areas for improvement, ask when he would like to schedule a follow-up meeting to assess your progress.

ⓘ *NT Tip*

If you experience significant, repeated problems meeting expectations, you may be in the wrong job. Does your position emphasize your areas of challenge instead of maximizing your strengths? Are you regularly redoing assignments, missing deadlines or working significantly longer hours than your peers? "How to Tell if You are in the Wrong Job or Career" is covered in Chapter 7.

- *Accept that you will need to work within employer guidelines*, even if they don't make sense to you. This is part of being a team player. Perfectionism and black-and-white thinking can get in the way of performance.

Greg had a rigid definition of his role as a programmer. Less than two months in a new position, he had angered every one of his colleagues in the IT department. Greg considered his job to be building the finest, most sophisticated systems possible. Convinced that he knew the best and right way, Greg refused to accept the project parameters.

"I've explained to Greg several times that we have three months to complete this project, and have a fixed budget," his exasperated supervisor explained. "What Greg is proposing would take a couple of years to build, and cost far more than what the company can afford."

Greg continued to defend his vision. "What I've developed is more robust, and will revolutionize the way the company manages data," he said.

While that may have been true, it was also true that the company's need was for an easy-to-implement solution. Greg focused on his idea of what was important, instead of his employer's business need. Unfortunately, Greg was not able to adjust and accept the employer's perspective, and chose to leave the company.

Businesses exist to make a profit. To do this, they must produce products or services that meet the needs of their customers, at a cost that allows them to be profitable. Working as part of a team sometimes means compromising your vision for the good of the organization.

Understand Your Learning Style

Learning style refers to the way in which an individual learns best. The three primary learning styles are visual, auditory and tactile/kinesthetic (Tileston 2004). A person may have a clear preference for one style, or prefer a combination of two or all three styles.

There are many free online tests that can help you determine your learning style. The website of LD Pride (www.ldpride.net) also includes information about Multiple Intelligence and learning disorders. The VARK guide to learning styles site (www.vark-learn.com) offers a brief questionnaire that you can fill out to learn your preferred style.

- *Visual learners* prefer to see information presented in words, diagrams or pictures. They learn best with detailed notes and written outlines, as well as charts, photographs and diagrams. Color-coding and the use of visual reminders, like sticky notes and icons, are useful aids for organizing work and remembering tasks.

- *Auditory learners* prefer to hear information. They learn best by attending lectures, participating in group discussions, and listening to spoken and recorded instructions. Several of my NLD clients, who have a strong preference for auditory learning, have to talk themselves through a process or procedure in order to understand it.

- *Tactile/kinesthetic learners* are literally "hands-on." They enjoy participating in demonstrations, making models or learning while doing, such as by operating a piece of machinery. Writing each step of a process on separate index cards, and then arranging the cards into the correct sequence, is a strategy for remembering a multistep process.

A person who prefers auditory *and* visual learning might listen to instructions first, and then refer to written text. Someone who is a visual and tactile learner might read about a procedure, and then try the steps himself.

You can use the knowledge of how you learn best to explain how you need to be trained. I have had clients who made accommodation requests based on their preferred method of processing information. An example is asking for written materials in place of verbal instructions.

PROJECTING CONFIDENCE

Although she had only been at her job for two weeks, Ally's supervisor and co-workers frequently asked whether she was "okay." At work, she would bite her fingernails, look at colleagues with a wide-eyed, frightened expression, and stand with her arms wrapped tightly around her body. Ally believed that because she was getting her assignments completed on time, her anxiety was not a concern.

Ron described himself as *reeking* of low self-confidence. After four years as senior project manager at his current company, Ron wanted a promotion to director of information systems.

Ron was intimidated when he had to give presentations to the senior management team. "I feel inferior to them," he said, "and then I get flustered and start rambling." If his ideas or conclusions were challenged, Ron would freeze and say, "I don't know." On several occasions, his colleagues told him that he was being too sensitive. His boss once described him as "high maintenance" because of his repeated requests for reassurance. During one meeting, a colleague said that he did not understand one of Rob's recommendations. Rob interpreted the comment as an attack, and replied, "I'm not illiterate!"

Ron rarely acknowledged the contributions of his colleagues, because he thought that sharing credit would diminish his accomplishments.

Lack of confidence was getting in the way of Ally and Ron reaching their goals. Neurotypicals experience self-doubt, too. However, they are usually better at disguising their inner feelings.

Many individuals with Asperger's Syndrome have long histories of being teased, bullied, ostracized, and placed into bad work situations. These experiences chip away at self-confidence and self-esteem. The daily stress of trying to interpret the reactions or expectations of other people can further diminish a sense of competence.

Even if you do not feel confident on the inside, you can act in ways that project self-assurance. This is not dishonest. It is a way to influence how your colleagues perceive you. At work, it is important that you are perceived as capable of working independently, making good decisions, and handling unexpected situations.

The following behaviors suggest low confidence, and will raise doubts about your abilities:

- talking too quickly or too softly; mumbling

- looking away from people.

- over-reacting to minor mistakes or criticism with anger, defensiveness, guilt or recrimination

- asking too many questions, or the same question, about something you already know

- repeatedly asking for validation that you did a good job

- not participating in meetings

- offering a weak handshake, crossing your arms across your chest, appearing to have very stiff muscles.

There is a difference between healthy self-confidence and arrogance. Arrogant people have an exaggerated opinion of their ability, importance, or the significance of their accomplishments. They consider themselves superior. Usually, they are not.

Confident people realistically assess their strengths and their weaknesses. They seek out ideas from others, and are not afraid to share credit. Instead of relying on what they already know, they are always learning (Gebelein *et al.* 1996). Confident people are willing to accept feedback. When they make a mistake, they learn from it and move on.

These are suggestions for building and projecting confidence at work:

- *Set realistic goals and expectations.* Nothing will crush confidence faster than striving for a goal that you cannot attain. Check that you have, or can acquire, the knowledge, skills and resources needed to achieve your aim. Be sure that your expectations are reasonable. I have worked with clients whose expectations about salary, the position they qualify for, or how other people should act are completely unrealistic. They quickly become frustrated and feel bad about themselves. Refer to the SMART goals planner in Chapter 5 for guidance on reasonable goals.

- *Use confident body language.* Smile and look people in the eye when you greet them. Speak in a clear voice, at a rate that others can easily understand. Do not fiddle with your hair or objects, or make exaggerated gestures. If you make verbal presentations, make a video recording of a practice session to analyze your body language, or ask a colleague for feedback.

- *Dress for success.* When I teach about nonverbal communication, I show a picture of a 1960s-era hippie. The man has shoulder-length hair, held back with a macramé headband. Small, wire-rimmed glasses sit at the end of his nose. He is wearing a tie-dyed T-shirt, and making the peace sign. People laugh when I show this photo, within the context of the workplace, because it is so obviously out of place. However, it illustrates how physical appearance creates an immediate, powerful impression.

  Dressing for success means selecting personal attire that makes you look professional and competent, and that is appropriate for your line of work. If you work for an investment bank and are male, you will be expected to wear a suit and tie. At a technology start-up in Silicon Valley, professional dress would be a dress shirt and pants.

  If you are uncertain about how to put together a professional wardrobe, ask a sales associate at a department or clothing store for advice. Good quality, reasonably fashionable clothing is worth the investment. When you look confident, you feel confident.

- *Avoid qualifiers.* These are phrases that diminish the conviction of what you say or write: "I thought that maybe…" or "I may be wrong, but…" or "This is probably a crazy idea…" Use definitive language: "My plan is…" or "The direction I propose is…"

- *Let go of perfection.* "Perfect" is an impossible standard. People tell me that they won't try something new because they might make a mistake. Yet, mistakes are how people learn. Try thinking of each mistake you make as moving you closer to mastery. Put slip-ups in the proper perspective: most errors are not catastrophic. If you make a mistake, do not blame others or make excuses. Find a solution and move on to something else.

- *Go for small wins.* Success builds confidence. Set yourself up to succeed with small, manageable goals.

- *Practice.* Just reading or thinking about how to do something won't build your skill. Plan consistent practice periods. Several short periods are usually more effective than one, marathon session. For example, set a timer for five or ten minutes and practice a greeting or making definitive statements. Repeat this twice a day for a week and assess your progress.

Building confidence is a process that happens over time. What I notice is that people give up too quickly. Expect that things will not always go according to plan. If one thing doesn't work, try another. *Believe* that you can improve, otherwise you will have little impetus for action.

CHAPTER 4

PEOPLE SKILLS

In addition to coaching individuals, I provide services to organizations. When an employer contacts me for a consultation or employee coaching, I almost invariably hear, "This employee's job skills are excellent. The problem is people skills."

People skills refers to the way people interact with each other. Listening, collaborating, sharing ideas, influencing, negotiating, motivating others, and managing conflicts are examples of people skills. They relate to working effectively within a group.

As I mentioned in the first chapter of this book, it is my experience that "people skills" account for the majority of difficulties that Aspergians have on the job. The most common problem areas for my clients are:

- not listening to instructions, or going outside the parameters of a project

- perseverating on a matter that has already been discussed and decided

- alienating co-workers with comments that are considered to be rude, disrespectful or demeaning

- acting out with emotional outbursts of anger or frustration

- dominating meetings by talking too much, or continually interrupting others

- frequently challenging or resisting the ideas of others; always needing to be right

- insisting on doing things a certain way, even if this lessens overall productivity

- claiming discrimination, harassment, or civil rights violations when challenged in any way, and when none has occurred.

Behaviors like these are disruptive, and lower team morale and productivity. They will cause co-workers to avoid you. They can cost you your job or a promotion. This chapter offers suggestions for handling potentially difficult situations so that they do not interfere with your job performance.

ACCEPTING FEEDBACK AND CRITICISM

"I don't take criticism well and I'll dig in my heels if I don't want to do something. That will frustrate anyone who tries to manage me." (Manufacturer's Representative, age 39)

To be a successful employee, you must be able to accept feedback that is given to you and deal constructively with criticism.

Without feedback, you wouldn't know where your job performance is strong and where you need to make improvements. It is part of a manager's job to provide positive and negative feedback to the people who report to him. Most companies have a formal schedule of when managers provide feedback to employees, usually during an annual or semi-annual performance review. Managers also receive feedback, at their performance reviews, and via 360-degree feedback surveys. These surveys are given to the manager's peers, superiors and subordinates (thus the name "360" or "full circle" input) who answer questions about the manager's abilities and areas for development or improvement.

Criticism is the unfavorable evaluation of a project, task or behavior. Although the terms "negative feedback" and "criticism" can be used interchangeably, I think of criticism as a concrete directive about something specific that an individual needs to change: "There are too many errors in this report." Feedback is guidance about how to enhance your performance: "You need to prioritize better and keep me and team members informed about project status."

I make a distinction between feedback and criticism for a reason. Clients frequently share their performance reviews with me. It is not uncommon that "difficulty accepting criticism" is noted as an area for improvement. Often, the individual challenges his supervisor about the criticism, denying that it is true, or trying to justify his actions. This can have negative consequences.

The first thing to do if you receive criticism is to listen to what is being said, and try to understand why the person needed to say it. Do not take it as a personal affront or attack. Perhaps, you do not understand expectations or need additional training. Maybe you need to work on your communication skills or learn how to follow someone else's rules. Criticism provides you the opportunity to make the changes and be successful.

Many of my clients confuse feedback with criticism and take it very personally. As a result, they miss the real message and focus their energy on changing the wrong thing. William's performance review described two areas for improvement. He was asked to summarize the main points during presentations, instead of providing a lot of detail, and to use language that nontechnical personnel could understand. William, who was hoping for a promotion, thought that the review was very negative.

"This is saying that I can't advance," he said.

"No," I replied, "it is telling you *how* to advance."

Once he could see the feedback as a roadmap for his development, we were able to focus on how William could adjust his presentations to sell his ideas to an executive audience.

Feedback provides insight into how other people perceive you. You then have the chance to influence or change those perceptions by continuing to do more of what is working, and changing what is not.

You are making an impression on the people you work with every day. Even if their perceptions do not represent your views of the truth of the situation, they do represent that person's experience. A person's experience is their truth. This is important to know because people will treat you based on how they perceive you. An individual who is perceived as friendly but "eccentric" will be treated differently than one who is perceived as unfriendly and strange. Unless you are aware of the impression you are making on others, you can't do anything to change it.

This is why you should listen to feedback without becoming defensive. After Jeff learned that his colleagues found him to be very critical, he changed the way that he spoke to others. His colleagues noticed the change and after a few months, came to welcome Jeff's thoughtful suggestions.

How to use criticism and feedback constructively:

- *Do not interrupt*, or begin questioning the validity of what you are hearing, or attempt to justify your point of view.

- *Listen carefully and take notes*. Ask questions to clarify what you don't understand.

- *Think about why people perceive you as they do.* Get help with this if necessary from your work buddy or supervisor, or a professional such as a therapist or coach. Have you received similar criticism or feedback before? If so, it is something to take seriously. Can you see how the reactions of others make sense within the context of the situation?

- *Decide specific actions* that you can take to change people's perceptions, or address their criticisms.

- *Be consistent with your actions.* Over time, people's impressions can change.

BEING CRITICAL OF OTHERS

Some individuals with Asperger's Syndrome are very critical of others. They have high expectations of how people should act. They become agitated if a person doesn't react in the way they expect. They feel justified in pointing out mistakes, in front of other co-workers. They dismiss ideas before the other person has finished explaining them. Individuals who the Aspergian believes are less intelligent are looked down upon.

Lisa is an engineer at a large, multinational firm. Her intellect and technical ability won her two promotions within five years. When an opportunity came up to lead a team on a new design project, she approached her supervisor immediately.

They discussed the project and the role of the lead engineer. Her boss let Lisa know that other staff members were being considered for the assignment. Still, Lisa believed that the job was hers. She was passionate about her work, smarter than most of her colleagues, and had been promoted.

Several weeks later, Lisa was told that a co-worker won the assignment. She was shocked to learn why. Lisa had been described by her colleagues as condescending and unsupportive. At issue were her blunt remarks about their subpar work and "silly" ideas. After delivering the bad news, her supervisor suggested that Lisa speak to a human resources manager about leadership training.

"I don't want to be unsupportive," Lisa said, "but I have to be honest with the people on my team. If their ideas are no good, I need to say so. Now the company is telling me to lie."

Lisa believed that her co-workers didn't grasp complex engineering problems quickly because they didn't try hard, or were "stupid." It hadn't occurred to her that some individuals simply needed more time to process information, or additional training. I wondered aloud whether some didn't speak up to avoid being interrupted and told why their thinking was wrong—in front of their peers.

We discussed the strengths of each team member. Lisa began to see how personal qualities such as thoroughness, creativity, and a willingness to experiment also contributed to the success of a project. She did some reading and learned that good leaders find ways to utilize people's strengths, rather than pointing out their weaknesses.

It is the responsibility of an individual's supervisor to judge the quality of someone's work and their method for completing it. If you need to point out an error, or believe that there is a better way to handle a task, address the *issue*, don't be critical of the *person*. Describe the event in factual terms. Avoid judgments about an individual's motives or abilities.

Wrong way to point out an error: "You didn't focus, and made four mistakes."

Right way to point out an error: "There are errors in spelling and punctuation on pages three and six."

Wrong way to suggest a change: "This process is ridiculous and inefficient. Here is how to make it better…"

Right way to suggest a change: "There seem to be extra steps in the process. My suggestion is to…"

Be sure that there is a business basis for your criticism, not a personal one, such as perfectionism or dislike of change.

There are examples of how to confront others in a professional way later in this chapter in the section called "Conflicts and Disagreements."

DEALING WITH AUTHORITY

"Making a list of people and their roles in the workplace helps me remember the levels of respect due managers and the camaraderie due peers." (Food Service Worker and Educator, age 56)

Peter came to see me because he was unhappy with his performance review. Peter felt that he had done an outstanding job over the prior year and was expecting an excellent evaluation and a raise. His supervisor saw Peter's performance differently. Peter was described as difficult to work with and unable to prioritize projects. He was also taken to task for not keeping colleagues informed about project delays.

As we went over Peter's employment history, a pattern emerged. In his previous jobs, he had experienced significant conflict with his supervisor and other senior members of the organization. Often the conflicts became serious enough that Peter was fired or chose to resign before being let go. "What am I missing?" he asked.

Difficulty dealing with authority can become a chronic problem that results in multiple job losses. As resumes grow longer, with one short-term position after another, it gets harder and harder to explain why employment lasts months instead of years, and to find a new job.

Sometimes, you have to work for an unreasonable, difficult boss. Individuals can be promoted into supervisory roles because they excel at technical aspects of their jobs, not because they are skilled at managing others. Office politics can also put people in positions of authority for which they are not ready or qualified. Supervisors can overuse their authority, have poor communication skills (yes, even neurotypicals can have problems with communication!) or be overwhelmed by their responsibilities.

However, if it seems to you that *all* of your bosses are jerks, the problem is probably with you. Your supervisor does not work in a vacuum; he or she has a boss, too. There are times when managers must implement policies, even though they don't agree with them. If there is a productivity problem in your department, the supervisor is accountable and is expected to fix it.

If conflict with people in authority has become an ongoing problem for you, or you are concerned that it will be, the reason might be one or more of the following:

- *Belief that your boss doesn't deserve your respect because you are intellectually superior.* The problem with this attitude is that success in the neurotypical workplace is almost always more dependent on getting along with others than on raw intelligence. Your supervisor will probably sense your contempt and be even less inclined to want to work with you. Over time, he may want to fire you. Focus on cultivating workplace communication skills, such as treating others with respect, being cooperative and working well on a team.

- *Continually questioning or challenging assignments.* You must accept that it is your supervisor's role to direct the activities of the people reporting to him or her. Generally, the less complex the job, the more control the supervisor has over how it will be done. Even in cases where it is acceptable to question an assignment, for example, if you have a manager-level position, you must choose your battles. Be sure to differentiate suggesting a legitimate improvement and simply wanting to do something your own way.

- *Treating your supervisor as an enemy.* Coming into work each day prepared for battle makes it almost certain that you will find one. There are clients who tell me in great detail about how unreasonable, mean and uncaring their supervisor is, despite the fact that this same supervisor has given them a promotion or raise. Just because your supervisor doesn't handle a situation the way that you want, it doesn't mean that they are wrong or being mean. You may be misinterpreting the situation or the manager's actions, or be overreacting based on your anxiety.

    Max called his supervisor abusive for denying him a day off. The supervisor was making sure that there would be enough personnel in the office to service customers. Max's behavior was inappropriate, because his supervisor's responsibility was to make sure that staffing levels were adequate.

    ### ⓘ *NT Tip*
    If you are having difficulties with your boss, try to find out if other people in your department are having problems with the boss, too. Pick one or two people who you trust and raise the subject in a subtle way. You might say, "I've been getting a lot of criticism from Mike about the time it takes me to finish the reports. Have you had this problem, too?"

- *Treating your supervisor like a peer.* Even if the standard in your workplace is to address your supervisor by his first name, some degree of deference is expected. Observe how other people in your department, particularly your peers, interact with the supervisor. Be particularly sensitive about avoiding behaviors that could embarrass your supervisor in front of others, like pointing out an error, or that bring your loyalty into question, such as criticizing a decision.

- *Refusing to do something because you think it is dumb.* Instead of ignoring a request or bluntly stating your opposing opinion, try to understand why the request was made. Use language *and a tone of voice* that express curiosity, not condemnation: "You want me to use the copy machine at the end of the hall. I'm curious why I can't use the one near my desk?" or "It seems redundant for both Bill and me to review the statistics. Is there a reason that it is handled that way?" Do not question every request or decision, or it will appear that you are challenging your supervisor's authority, leadership, and managerial skills. If you are new on the job, learn the existing system first. You might come to understand reasons behind the way things are done that initially don't make sense to you.

DEALING WITH CHANGE

Most people dislike change.

Most people with Asperger's Syndrome dislike change *a lot*. This makes perfect sense to me. The world often seems so random and confusing, it is natural that you would prefer that the work environment remains stable, consistent and predictable.

The problem is that work environments are always changing. Employees leave and new ones are hired to take their place. Individuals get promoted and corporate hierarchies are restructured. Companies are sold, merged and acquired. Growth means adding employees and changing roles and responsibilities. New technologies can render jobs or processes obsolete. Budgets get cut and business priorities shift.

After 11 years of working together, Richard's supervisor retired. A new manager was hired from another company. Over the next few months, she instituted many changes that affected how Richard's job was performed. For example, she expected Richard and his two fellow web content managers to proofread content, implement search engine optimization strategies, and work with the marketing team to improve product sales. Budget cuts eliminated the freelance help that Richard was accustomed to accessing.

Richard's former supervisor was casual and laid back. His new manager was business-like and demanding. "She thrives on stress," Richard explained, "and stress makes me shut down."

And shut down he did. He began ignoring tasks that he didn't understand. Instead of implementing his manager's suggestions for streamlining his work, Richard continued doing things as he always had. As his stress built, he withdrew into himself, no longer talking to his co-workers. Richard and his new manager became increasingly frustrated with each other. He was put on a formal performance improvement plan (PIP).

Change can create feelings of uncertainty, anxiety, anger, confusion, fear and sadness. Some of the ways that people resist change include:

- continuing to work as they have previously

- refusing to see any benefits of change

- pointing out why the change won't work

- incessantly questioning the need for change

- sabotaging the change with passive-aggressive behaviors like "forgetting" what to do, or acting confused about what needs to happen.

Resisting change is ineffective, creates conflict, and can potentially lead to job loss.

Many clients say that they were "blindsided" by change (they didn't see it coming). Resignations, layoffs and reorganizations sometimes do occur without warning. Usually, though, there are signs of a change coming that the person with Asperger's Syndrome doesn't notice.

Industry trends may hint at the possibility of layoffs or even the demise of a company. When multiple firms compete in crowded, mature markets, some will not survive. An aggressive rival or a cutting-edge technology can siphon sales and market share, reducing profitability. Regulatory changes dictate how companies in your industry do business. If competitors are outsourcing jobs to cut costs and remain competitive, your company might be forced to do so as well. This is why staying informed about industry trends is a good idea.

ⓘ *NT Tip*
Nearly every occupation has at least one professional association. This is an organization comprised of individuals who work in the same field. Associations keep their members apprised of news

and trends that affect their jobs, and facilitate networking. The internet makes it easy to locate professional associations.

When your company's executives have frequent, closed-door meetings, this usually indicates major changes are being planned. The resignations of several executives or department heads can mean your company is in financial difficulty. If consultants have been brought in to review the business, it may be because it will soon be put up for sale. When your supervisor asks frequently for reports about current and projected sales, marketing plans, and expenses, this indicates concerns about losing sales and market share or decreased profitability. A company rumor mill in overdrive often signals changes coming, although what is rumored is not always accurate.

Change can be visible to an employee. Has your manager been preoccupied or spending a lot of time with a peer in your department? Have you been excluded from meetings or pulled off major projects? These can be signs that your manager is getting promoted or leaving the company; a peer is being groomed for a new role; a reorganization is taking place; or your job is in jeopardy.

Do not panic or make assumptions if you suspect that change is coming. Talk over the situation with someone you trust, like your work buddy. Do not project your thoughts too far into the future. You may have misread signs or the rumors might be wrong. Continue to do your work to the best of your ability and avoid taking part in the rumor mill.

When a change is announced, do not panic or make assumptions, either. Listen carefully to what is said and take notes. People often fear change because they:

- are uncertain about what to expect from a new manager

- have concerns about losing their jobs after a company acquisition, merger or sale

- doubt that a change is needed or desirable

- believe that there must be negative consequences coming

- fear that they will lose something of personal value, such as status, power, prestige, authority, security, perks or benefits

- are afraid to take the risk of learning something new, reporting to a different supervisor, or assuming a different role

- worry they do not possess the knowledge, skills or abilities to succeed in the new environment

- don't consider that change also creates opportunities.

Rather than waste your energy resisting the inevitable, take constructive action to adapt. Look for similarities between your work situation before and now. What knowledge, skills and experience can you carry over to the new situation or to a new employer? What can you can do to fit in to new circumstances? If the organization has a new management team or you have a new supervisor, listen carefully to their priorities and goals. If you lack needed skills or knowledge, come up with a plan for acquiring them.

Ask questions when you are uncertain about what you should do differently. In large group meetings, limit your questions to topics which pertain to the interests of everyone. Save specific concerns about your job for your supervisor and your work buddy.

New managers often ask employees what they would like to change about their jobs or about the company. Frame your responses in a constructive way. Your words and actions are making an impression on people. Negative, judgmental and cynical comments will portray you as an angry, unmotivated employee. Your commitment to the company will be questioned. Compare the following examples of constructive and combative comments:

Constructive: "I see some inefficiency between our group and the sales department."

Combative: "The sales people are always late turning in their orders and slow down the processing cycle."

Constructive: "I would like to be more involved with the planning of marketing campaigns."

Combative: "I am completely bored with my current job."

Constructive: "For several months, we have been discussing a new order entry system."

Combative: "We've been complaining for months about the outdated order entry system."

Refrain from making disapproving comments about a current or former supervisor, members of the management team or your co-workers. This will have people wondering why *you* can't get along with others. Bottom line: managers want enthusiastic, positive, dedicated people on their team.

Do not resist if you are asked to handle an aspect of your job differently or take on new responsibilities. Treat this as a chance to learn something new that might make your job easier, more interesting, or secure. You may be tested to see if you will fit in, or about a potential promotion. Do not talk about how you used to do things or why the old way was better. It makes you appear unwilling to change.

If you have a new supervisor, pay particular attention to his work style. Does he prefer face-to-face meetings or rely mostly on email? Does he like written or verbal status reports? How often does he want to be updated, and in how much detail? If the answers to these questions are not obvious to you, ask: "How would you like me to update you?" or "What is enough detail and what is too much?"

Organizations are comprised of groups of people who have disparate backgrounds. They come together for the purpose of contributing their skills to reach a common goal. Cordial and respectful relationships make that process easier and less stressful for everyone.

CONFLICTS AND DISAGREEMENTS

Dan was considered a brilliant engineer and was respected for his vast knowledge of his company's products and internal processes. Co-workers commented that Dan always seemed to be two or three steps ahead of them, able to quickly size up a proposal and determine whether it was feasible. A 16-year veteran of the organization, Dan had amassed a wealth of institutional knowledge and could recall facts that others had long forgotten.

Two years before, the company had gone through a major reorganization. Dan had never fully been able to adapt to the changes in management and culture. Although he reported to the same supervisor, Dan worked on an almost daily basis with a manager he did not like or respect. Dan believed that the manager deliberately tried to make him look incompetent. The manager would promise to get information to Dan by a certain date and not deliver. Their philosophies about product design were quite different and their discussions sometimes turned into shouting matches.

Dan was also expected to collaborate with product development, marketing, and sales personnel. Their lack of basic engineering knowledge frustrated Dan to the point that he would lose his temper, curse, or simply walk out of meetings. He would routinely preface answers to a colleague's questions with, "I can't believe you don't know that" or "You've worked here long enough to know…"

His second post-reorganization performance review was a complete shock to Dan. He was told that he would not receive a long-anticipated promotion because of his abrasive interpersonal style. "It isn't so much what you say as how you say it," his supervisor said. "People feel that they are being criticized and belittled. You need to be collaborating."

Jill was one of two paralegals in a small law firm. She and her peer, Susan, each worked for two attorneys and were expected to help each other with assignments when the firm was busy. Jill didn't particularly like Susan, who was loud, careless with her work. and prone to taking extra long lunch breaks. Still, they had managed to work together for nearly a year without incident.

One afternoon Allen, an attorney, asked Jill if she knew where Susan was. "She's at lunch," Jill replied. "Oh?" said Allen, looking at his watch. "Would you tell her to stop by my office as soon as she gets in?" he asked.

After he left, Jill looked at her watch and noticed that it was 1:40pm. Susan had left for lunch at about 12:15pm. She was already almost a half hour late.

When Susan finally came in at about 1:50pm, Jill relayed the conversation with Allen. "Why did you tell him I was at lunch?" Susan asked in an angry tone, "Now he's going to be mad because I'm late. Thanks a lot," she added and stormed off.

The exchange left Jill anxious and upset. Why wouldn't she tell Allen that Susan was at lunch, if that's where she was? Why was Susan so angry at her for being honest? Jill had no idea what to do next and spent 15 minutes crying in the ladies' room.

Disagreements are a common part of working life. They can range in intensity from minor differences of opinion to major conflicts. The causes can be many. In Dan's case, the way he spoke caused his colleagues to think that he didn't respect them. Jill had a misunderstanding with Susan, who wrongly assumed that Jill had told Allen when she had left for lunch. Allen had seen Susan leaving the building at a quarter past noon.

Differing personality styles can cause friction between co-workers, as can contradictory goals and divergent values. The goal of the research department might be to produce an in-depth, insightful report. The goal of the marketing department might be to have a finished report to sell. Any delays will cause tension between the two departments. The people in research will feel pressured to produce a product that is not comprehensive. The people in marketing will feel that the researchers are taking too long and holding up sales and promotion. The vice president might value quick, decisive decision-making while his manager values the careful evaluation of lots of data. The vice president will be impatient with the manager, and the manager will feel pressured by the vice president.

Whether disagreements can be resolved before they become emotionally charged conflicts depends on a number of factors. Unrealistic expectations or conflicting directives from senior executives can create workplaces that are filled with fear and mistrust. In-fighting between department or division heads can stall projects and lead to anger, hurt feelings, and ongoing rivalry.

There is nothing you can do about management conflicts, unless you are at the same management level. However, there are techniques that you can learn to handle disagreements and conflicts between you and your co-workers.

The purpose of your interactions with others is the fulfillment of business objectives. You do not need to personally like a colleague in order to work with him, nor do you have to agree with everything he says or does. Be prepared to interact with people whose perspectives, personalities, goals and values differ from yours.

Keep in mind the social orientation of neurotypicals. They do not want to look foolish, especially in front of staff members and their boss. Within a group, they often seek consensus, and will compromise to maintain harmony. Dan, like many of my clients, didn't think about this and, as a result, his manager and colleagues felt belittled and criticized.

It is okay to disagree with co-workers, give them feedback or challenge their ideas, as long as you are not overstepping your authority. Examples of overstepping authority include:

- ignoring company policies or procedures

- performing tasks that are not in your job description

- giving instructions to people who do not report to you

- criticizing the performance of people who do not report to you

- offering unsolicited comments or advice about projects in other departments

- attempting tasks for which you do not have the skills or experience

- refusing to accept direction from your supervisor or a member of senior management

- bringing minor disagreements to your supervisor before trying to work them out with the individual involved

- undermining your supervisor's authority by saying negative things about him to co-workers.

When you give feedback or disagree, avoid statements that imply judgment, or that reflect your opinion about what happened and how you or others reacted. The statement, "If you had listened to the instructions, we would have been done by now," implies judgment of an individual. The unspoken meaning is, "If you had done what you were supposed to, the project would have been completed on time." The statement, "No one could understand your logic," is evaluative. It implies that others share this opinion because the presenter didn't articulate his thoughts well.

Statements that imply judgment or that are evaluative make people defensive. Instead of hearing the content of your message, they concentrate on protecting themselves from a perceived attack. *If your words don't make people defensive, they are able to listen to what you have to say.*

To do this, state your opinions or beliefs using neutral language and "I" statements rather than "you" statements: "I see it a different way;" or "I hear what you are saying, but my experience is different;" or "Let me share my concerns." You can also ask questions to better understand someone's thinking or point of view: "How do you see that working?" or "How did you arrive at that conclusion?" or "What would it take to implement that plan?"

Unresolved disagreements and conflicts can worsen over time, so it is important to take action to correct the situation. Speak directly with the individual first, in a private location. The following five-step model outlines an effective way to give someone feedback in a non-judgmental way.

- Step 1: Describe the situation using specific, *factual* (not judgmental or evaluative) language.

- Step 2: Describe what impact the situation has on the project or company.

- Step 3: Explain how the situation affects you and your work.

- Step 4: Explain, in detail, what you would have the person do differently.

- Step 5: Ask for agreement.

Dan used this model the next time that his manager did not follow through with promised information:

"When the specs are late…" (factual description)

"I have to revise the plan for the review committee…" (impact of situation)

"This takes about an hour of my time…" (effect on you)

"Please give deadlines you are certain you can meet…" (what you want the person to do)

"Is this reasonable?" (ask for agreement)

Do not omit the last step. People are more likely to follow through if they agree with what they are being asked to do. This question gives the other person a chance to raise their concerns so that the situation can be resolved.

Practice this model until you are comfortable with it. You do not have to use the exact phrasing in the example. Use words that feel natural to you. If you sound disingenuous or rehearsed, people will not respond favorably. It can be helpful to write down what you want to say and practice it a few times.

> ⓘ **NT Tip**
> It is imperative that your words sound genuine and convey an intention to resolve a conflict or disagreement. If you are unsure about how you sound to others, use a tape recorder to practice stating opinions and giving feedback in the right way.

This kind of feedback should be given within 24 hours of an incident. Unless there is a very specific or important reason for doing so, avoid bringing up events that happened days or weeks ago. This can make it seem like you are harping on the past or intentionally trying to demean someone.

If your efforts to resolve the situation are not successful, or you are unsure about what to do, speak with your supervisor or work buddy. Use factual, neutral language: "I'm confused about a situation with Bill" or "Jane and I don't see eye to eye and it's affecting our projects."

When Susan returned from her meeting with Allen, she apologized to Jill for the misunderstanding. Jill accepted the apology, grateful to know that she had not done anything wrong. Still concerned, Jill spoke with her supervisor and they agreed that if Susan did something similar in the future, Jill would let her supervisor know.

CONFLICT…OR MISUNDERSTANDING?

If a co-worker says or does something that upsets you, it might be a misunderstanding. There are many reasons why misunderstandings occur. Before you react, or accuse someone of negative intentions, see if one of the following applies.

- *Taking things personally.* This is when you assume that the words and actions of others are directed at you specifically. Janice was convinced that her boss "hated" her because he denied her a certain day off. However, the decision had nothing to do with his personal feelings toward her; the department was implementing new order processing software, and training was scheduled for that day.

  Low self-esteem can cause a person to perceive innocent behavior as a put-down or attack. Peter often became very angry when his supervisor corrected errors. "He thinks that I'm stupid," Peter fumed. After working with a therapist, he realized that he was taking the corrections personally, due to his negative beliefs about himself.

- *Misinterpreting an action or remark.* This is especially likely if you have difficulty interpreting situational context, or decoding the meaning of a person's tone of voice, facial expression, or body language. Nan was told by her manager to assist a co-worker in another part of the building. When Nan arrived, the co-worker asked, "Why are you here?" Nan thought her co-worker was intimating that she didn't think Nan should have her job. When we dissected the interaction, it was clear that the co-worker wasn't expecting Nan to assist her with her projects that day.

- *Not considering context.* Think about the event, the people involved, and the reason for the interaction. How likely is it that the other person was making a joke, teasing you, or trying to be helpful? If you are not sure, ask: "I'm not sure what you mean;" or "Was that a joke?" or "I'm confused; are you upset about something?"

Put a single event or interaction into perspective. Get help with this if you need it. Think about your history with the other person. Is this individual usually friendly and helpful? Have you gotten along well in the past? Has a similar incident happened before? Everyone can have a bad day, so if behavior is out of character, it might be due to a personal or professional problem.

Put the severity of the event into perspective as well. Is it an inconsequential difference of opinion, a serious dispute…or something in between? Is it a minor incident that you need to handle yourself, or a major transgression that requires intervention from management?

If you are often angered, offended or hurt by others, the problem is likely to be that you are taking things personally, or misinterpreting situations. Think about working with a professional on how to become more objective and accurate in the way that you interpret events.

A PRIMER ON OFFICE POLITICS

"Politics is probably more important for success than you think it is." (IT Project Manager, age 62)

For many people, the term *office politics* conjures up images of a greedy, back-stabbing executive, who will do anything to get to the top, or the butt-kissing underling who wins a promotion, despite having no brains or talent. Although nearly everyone dislikes office politics, they participate in it anyway. The majority of people with Asperger's Syndrome find office politics to be thoroughly confusing and something to avoid.

Like it or not, office politics is a fact of working life. It is the unspoken rules about who has power in an organization, and how things get done. Yes, there are some people who play political games strictly for their own gain, often with poor results. Most employees just pay attention to these unspoken rules of organizational life because it makes their jobs easier.

It bears repeating that NTs are very focused on interpersonal relationships. Their group orientation means that struggles over where one fits within the hierarchy of the unit are common. This is why success at work requires more than having the talent and skills to do a job. Employees need to fit in to their organization's culture and figure out who has the power to get things done.

Like people, companies have their own personality, known as corporate culture. This does not necessarily match characteristics that are described in a marketing brochure or on a company's website. Corporate culture is based on shared values, which are the beliefs employees share about what is important. Values are what drive actions. You can learn a lot about company culture by observing what behaviors are rewarded. A company may claim to have a culture of innovation and creativity, yet it rewards consistency and preservation of the status quo.

It is possible for departments within a company to have distinct cultures that reflect the values of employees in that group, and not necessarily the values of the company. Managers have a tendency to hire people whose values and personalities are similar to their own. A bottom line oriented general manager is likely to hire staff members who will do whatever it takes to increase sales or profitability. One who is quality oriented will hire people who won't cut corners to meet sales targets. Neither culture is better or worse than the other; they are simply different. The first company might produce quality products, but bonuses are based on meeting sales targets. The second company might tolerate delays in order to release top-quality products. *Corporate culture rewards employees who most help the company succeed in the way most valued at that time.*

These are more types of contrasting company cultures:

- Hierarchical vs. collaborative.

- Emphasis on tasks and getting things done vs. interpersonal relationships and *how* things get done.

- Fixed rules and processes vs. flexible rules and processes.

- Business focus where people's private lives stay private vs. relationship-oriented where people have camaraderie on and off the job.

- Analytic, linear problem-solving vs. intuitive, creative problem-solving (Microsoft versus Apple).

- Slow-paced, static environment vs. fast-paced, rapidly changing environment.

A company's culture can change over time, sometimes dramatically. There may be a rapid influx of new employees due to fast growth, or a natural turnover of employees over several years. A significant event, such as a merger or acquisition, the death of a founder or other senior executive, hiring of a new CEO, regulatory change, or new market dynamics like greater price competition, can force a change in values.

Understanding office politics also means figuring out who has power and authority and how they use them to get things done. Job title can be an unreliable indicator of whether an individual has power or not. In every company there are two kinds of organizational charts. One is the official diagram that shows who reports to whom, the relationships between departments, and where responsibilities lie. The other, more important one, is the unofficial chain of command. This one reveals who has real authority. An individual's authority is typically based on who they know, their specialized expertise or institutional knowledge, or their ability to influence or help others. For example, a busy company president may give control of his calendar to his executive assistant. If you have dealings with the president, it helps to have a good relationship with his executive assistant, or you might find that meetings with the boss are hard to schedule.

Employees who possess specialized expertise may be given certain "perks" as an incentive to stay at the firm. Staff members who have worked at a company for many years amass a wealth of valuable institutional knowledge. Their power lies in their understanding of various processes, procedures, and people; in other words, how things really work. These are the individuals who make it their business to learn the needs of others in the organization. They use this information to influence the decisions of others, and increase their own influence.

OFFICE POLITICS IN ACTION

If you think that awareness of office politics is important only to people who work in big companies and want to climb the corporate ladder, think again. During high school, Mike had a part-time job at a local gas station. His passion was automobiles and he wanted desperately to learn how to fix them. During his breaks, Mike was in the garage, handing tools to the mechanics and watching them work. When he heard the station owner say, "I'm getting hungry," Mike offered to pick up lunch for him and the other mechanics (he did *not* pay for the lunches; he collected money from each person and walked to the sandwich shop to pick up the food when it was ready).

If Mike's motive had been disingenuous, helping the mechanics in order to get some kind of special treatment, it would have backfired. However, the station owner and the mechanics sensed his genuine interest in fixing cars. Even though he wasn't consciously aware of it, Mike used his understanding of who had power in the gas station to influence the right people. Instead of hanging out with the other pump attendants talking about sports, Mike built relationships with the mechanics and the owner of the station. That summer, Mike was working full time as a mechanic's apprentice.

Awareness of office politics tells you:

- who has the *real* authority

- how decisions get made

- what behaviors are rewarded

- what is really important

- who can champion your projects and ideas

- when and with whom you need to compromise.

As you begin to grasp these unspoken rules, events that seemed random or mystifying begin to make sense. You know who to go to for help. You stop taking the actions of others personally. The big picture becomes clearer: decisions that seemed contrary to stated business objectives make sense. You can see how people set themselves up for promotions by increasing their value to the company.

Katy and Suzanne worked as technical documentation writers for a large software company. Their job was to write clear, concise copy for manuals and online help that explain how to use a software product. The job required that they work closely with the developers who created the software.

Katy's writing skills were consistently described as excellent and exceeding expectations. Although she didn't work as quickly, her finished product was so thorough and accurate that it took little time to edit. Katy liked her job and each morning headed straight to her computer and began typing. She often ate lunch at her desk. She frequently got into heated debates with the developers about the features and functionality of their products. Katy admitted that she enjoyed these discussions. "I usually know more than they do, and win," she said.

Suzanne did not have the same depth of technical knowledge or writing skills. However, Suzanne got along well with both the developers and the editors, often joining them for lunch. She built relationships by filling them in on non-confidential information from the strategy meetings. Once, she stayed late to fix a big error that one of the editors made—before the supervisor could find out about it.

Company layoffs resulted in the loss of one editor and major cutbacks in the budget for freelance help. Everyone in the documentation department was feeling the pressure to get projects completed on time. It puzzled Katy that editors would stay late to work on Suzanne's projects, but not on hers. "My last two projects were for new product releases," Katy explained, "and that is where most of the revenue comes from. I don't understand why editors would waste extra time reviewing Suzanne's updates." The developers and editors were reciprocating for Suzanne's help by handling her projects first.

Katy also noticed that Suzanne was spending more and more time in closed-door meetings with Cory, the department supervisor. Suzanne was being invited to participate in monthly strategy meetings with the product and marketing managers. It was announced that Suzanne would accompany Cory to a major industry conference in the fall.

"Cory likes Suzanne and he doesn't like me," Katy said to Ellen, a junior editor with whom she was friendly. "That's why he's letting her go to the conference."

"Haven't you heard?" Ellen said, "Cory is taking a job in the product development group. Suzanne is going to be the documentation supervisor."

"I didn't see any announcement," Katy replied, stunned.

"There isn't going to be an announcement until next month," said Ellen. "Cory told two of the developers, and one of them told Ann in product development, who told me. Don't say anything, okay?"

On the surface, Suzanne's promotion seems absurd. Her writing and technical skills are not as strong as Katy's. She didn't work on the new product releases. She hadn't been at the company as long as Katy.

But, from the perspective of office politics, Suzanne's promotion makes perfect sense. She was perceived as a team player. The company culture placed a lot of value on group consensus and interaction, which Suzanne did well.

Cory noticed the good relationships that Suzanne had with her workmates. When he accepted a new position in the company, he immediately began grooming Suzanne to take over his job. The more politically astute members of the documentation department guessed that Suzanne's presence at the industry conference meant that she was going to get a promotion.

Even Ellen, who had only been with the company for five months, knew to utilize the company grapevine to find out news before it was announced. The grapevine is the information exchange that happens through informal networks.

Katy's lack of political awareness made it hard for her to influence others. As a result, her projects were not treated with the same sense of urgency as Suzanne's. It also kept her out of the running for a promotion. The software developers did not share Katy's enjoyment of the product debates. Several felt that she was condescending in her critiques and one had requested not to work with her in the future. By not joining her colleagues for lunch, Katy missed opportunities to form better relationships and learn more about their concerns and how she could help.

> ### ⓘ *NT Tip*
> Joining people in your department or work group for lunch is not a waste of time. The conversation may start off with small talk, but usually turns to business matters. It is part of "fitting in" and being "a team player."

Eric was chronically irritated by what he saw as capricious behavior by his colleagues. "The rules are not followed and arbitrarily broken at the whim of a co-worker or manager," he explained. What Eric didn't realize is that decisions can be politically motivated, and can appear contrary to stated business objectives. A manager who is in line for a promotion might decide to delay a not-quite-ready product release. A marketing director might support a sales department initiative because he knows that he will need help from the sales team. As in chess, people make moves and counter moves to win the game.

You may be wondering how, as a person with Asperger's Syndrome, you can ever hope to become savvy at office politics. You struggle to understand the motives of other people, often missing the implied meaning of what people say, and are uncomfortable with interpersonal interaction. It may seem that you have to lie about your motives, instead of saying what you really think.

You do not need to become a person who wields political power in your organization. Instead, you can develop enough awareness of office politics to make it easier to do your job. This can be as basic as making yourself available to help others who are behind on projects; taking an interest in what your colleagues are doing; and being supportive when they have professional or personal problems. In turn, your co-workers will do the same for you.

These are suggestions for increasing your awareness of office politics:

- *Become an astute observer.* Begin watching the daily interactions in the lunch room and during breaks to get an idea of who has interpersonal connections with whom. If necessary, keep a chart of people who frequently talk together (but be discreet about it). Pay attention to people in your own department. How do they act? Is there a lot of chatter and camaraderie or is everyone working silently at their desks? When people need answers or assistance, who do they go to for help? Who gets attention at meetings?

- *Look for people or situations that can help you,* once you understand the social networks. The peer who is friendly and patient when answering people's questions might be able to give you suggestions on how to work more efficiently.

- *Talk to people to learn about office politics.* Just be sure to do so in a politically correct way. Even though it is ubiquitous, company politicking is usually not openly acknowledged. Do not ask: "Who has the real power in this company?" or "What are the office politics like here?" Ask instead: "How would you describe the company's culture?" or "What are the primary concerns of the product development group?" or "What are the top three priorities over the next six months?"

- *Ask a co-worker you trust to act as your office politics interpreter.* This can be your work buddy, or other co-worker with whom you have developed a rapport. Be direct with your request: "I'm not good at office politics. Would you clue me in on how things work here?"

- *Accept that political motives, not logic, can drive decisions,* and use this awareness to learn when to compromise. If you rely only on official rules, policies, and procedures you will become frustrated.

- *Read business books that explain the dynamics of office politics.* Find one that you like and enlist the help of an NT to show you how to apply the concepts to your situation. If you are really inspired, study organizational development to gain insight into corporate culture.

WHAT IF THINGS GET UGLY?

A company's culture can become one of in-fighting, back-stabbing and never-ending political intrigue. Sometimes, innocent people get caught in the middle of the battles, and this can make the work environment very stressful and unproductive. Unless the politics directly affects your ability to do your work or your job security, try to stay out of the fray. It is likely that 99 percent of the gossip you hear will be wrong. Don't take sides; focus on your assigned tasks. There is very little that you can do to better the situation, and your best alternative may be to seek employment elsewhere.

Talk to someone, like a coach or career counselor, who can help you explore your options. Resist the urge to simply quit. It will make it harder for you to find another job, and make a bad impression on your current employer and co-workers. You never know when you could be working with a former colleague again. Whenever possible, leave an employer on good terms.

CHAPTER 5

EXECUTIVE FUNCTIONS AT WORK

Managing Time and Getting Things Done

"A big challenge in every way!" (Fiber Artist, age 50)

After less than a month, Martin was fired from a job as a retail sales associate. Although his full-scale IQ was in the superior range, he had been unable to find work related to his degree in finance. The retail position seemed like an easy way to earn money while he continued looking for a job in the financial field.

There were problems from the start. Martin had a hard time remembering and following the verbal instructions that he was given during the training period. He admitted that his "social judgment" was poor. He once called out, "We have an irate customer here," within earshot of the annoyed patron. He impulsively used his supervisor's computer without permission. When he had trouble completing a transaction, he didn't call his manager for help. Instead, he spent nearly half an hour trying to get the register to work, oblivious to the growing throng of impatient shoppers.

Mary was unable to estimate how long it would take to develop marketing materials, despite having more than 15 years of experience as a copywriter. She created schedules that were unrealistic, and spent too much time on low-priority tasks. Often, she started large, complex projects a day or two before they were due, resulting in errors and missed deadlines. Although the quality of her work was very good, Mary lost several jobs because she could not organize her work and meet deadlines.

Both Martin and Mary have deficits in executive functioning. *Executive function* refers to a broad array of cognitive processes that allow the efficient management of time and resources. A common analogy compares these processes to the activities of a business executive. Strong executive functioning enables an individual to:

- establish goals, and develop a realistic plan to reach them

- organize and prioritize tasks or information

- evaluate results, and decide on another course of action, if necessary

- shift back and forth, as needed, between the "big picture" and relevant details

- analyze information and draw conclusions

- see options, predict likely outcomes, and solve problems

- initiate tasks independently, and monitor results in relation to what is expected.

The ability to stop certain thoughts or activities is another aspect of executive function, known as inhibition. My clients who have difficulty with inhibition will surf the internet for extended periods of time, instead of attending to important projects. They stray from a primary task in order to follow interesting, yet irrelevant, tangents. Some impulsively act on a thought without considering the consequences (Cooper-Kahn and Dietzel 2008).

The very *concept* of time may be elusive for someone with executive function deficits. There is little awareness of how long a task will, or should, take; how quickly one needs to work in order to meet a deadline; or whether a time frame is realistic (e.g. "Can I complete this in 45 minutes?").

Clearly, executive functioning impacts job performance in many ways. Individuals vary in their profile of executive function strengths and deficits. This chapter offers suggestions for addressing the most common problems that I see in my coaching practice. I also recommend *Find Your Focus Zone* by Lucy Jo Palladino (2007).

WORKING MEMORY AND MULTITASKING

"Multitasking [is the biggest challenge] because I will be working on something and four other people need something else NOW." (Administrative Assistant, age 31)

Working memory functions as a kind of notepad in the brain. It is where information is made available for a short period of time, while you are working on a specific task (Cooper-Kahn and Dietzel 2008). It plays a critical role in learning, organizing written information, taking good notes, and responding to what someone has said or asked (Meltzer 2010). Recalling a telephone number long enough to actually make a call is an example of using working memory. So is remembering a sequence of three or four instructions: "Look up the account number, check to see when payment was made, let the customer know if their account is active, and close the file when done."

The amount of information that can be stored in the working memory is limited. The capacity for most people is seven pieces of information (Meltzer 2010). Most people are not able to solve a mathematical problem like this one in their heads: $443 \times 7 \div 9 - 31 + 1{,}558 = ?$ The amount of information needed to complete the computation exceeds working memory capacity. Additionally, stressors such as fatigue, interruptions, or distractions can result in the loss of information stored in the working memory (Gathercole and Alloway 2008).

Multitasking is an activity that requires strong working memory. When a person multitasks, he rapidly shifts his attention from one task to another. If you are speaking to someone on the telephone while writing a reply to an email, you are not literally doing both things at once. You are shifting your attention back and forth between the two.

Many of my clients report that when they are interrupted during a task, they lose their place, and have to start again from the beginning. The difficulty is not performing multiple job tasks, but having to switch quickly back and forth between them.

There are several ways to compensate for weak working memory, so that it does not interfere with your productivity:

- *Find a quiet workspace, and limit interruptions during the day.* Close your office door, or post a "do not disturb" sign outside of your cubicle, so that you can work uninterrupted for a period of time. If a co-worker interrupts you during an important task, ask to talk at a later time: "I am working on deadline right now; can we talk at 3:00?"

  ### ⓘ *NT Tip*
  In most workplaces it is expected that you *will* stop what you are doing if the interruption is from your supervisor, a senior executive, or a customer.

- *Schedule specific times during the day to check voicemail and email.* Turn off the email notification system on your computer. If you are distracted by sounds, wear noise-cancelling headphones, or use a white noise machine.

- *Write things down immediately*. You may want to carry a small pad for this purpose. Some people discover that they remember things better when they are written by hand, rather than keyed into an electronic device.

- *Create mnemonics*, such as rhymes and acronyms, to aid recall: "At the third light, I make a right" or "BAM! (Bring the Accounting files on Monday)."

- *"Chunk" information, by grouping pieces of data into categories*. Telephone numbers are a common example of chunking. The sequence 1905553210 is difficult to remember. When the digits are categorized into area code, prefix, and line number, recall is much easier: (190) 555-3210.

- *Use checklists* instead of relying on your memory.

- *Utilize electronic devices* to store information that you use frequently, schedule appointments, and remind yourself of commitments.

- *Develop routines, so that you lessen distractions*. Put your car keys in the same place; set out clothes for work the night before; visit the bank on the same day and time each week so that you always have enough cash for incidental expenses.

MANAGING TIME

"Unless someone tells me what needs to be done and by when, a project just doesn't seem real," said Matt. "So I forget about it until a day or two before it's due, and then I'm usually up all night working."

Alicia's problem was procrastination. "I don't know how to get started, so I keep putting things off until they are critical."

Many jobs require the ability to plan how and when tasks or assignments must be completed. This becomes difficult for individuals who:

- do not know how to get started (and do nothing)

- become stuck midway through a project

- underestimate how long a task will take

- miss certain steps, and then need to redo all or most of a project

- make a project more complex or detailed than it needs to be

- spend too much time on low-priority tasks.

Peter was excited to be assigned a special project, but could not find enough time to get started on it. He often complained about being the only person in his group who had to work late on a regular basis. When I asked Peter to describe how he spent his time during the day, he drew a blank.

The assignment I gave Peter was to track how long he spent on various tasks during the work day. He used a Daily Activity Log that divided the day into 15-minute increments (9:00am; 9:15am; 9:30am; 9:45am). Every day for two weeks, he noted what he was doing, when, and for how long. For example, on Monday, he attended a staff meeting from 10:00am to 10:30am. Then, he replied to emails from 10:30am to 11:15am.

In addition to tracking time spent, Peter rated the importance of the various tasks. A rating of C meant that the task was critical, and had to be done that day. A rating of I meant that the task was an important one, with a fixed deadline. Many of Peter's meetings were designated with an I. The L rating designated a low-priority item, which could be delegated to someone else, or that Peter could address whenever there was time.

After the two weeks were up, we reviewed Peter's log. He was shocked to discover that three to four hours per week were spent answering basic procedural questions from less experienced staff members, a low-priority task. He averaged two hours per day crafting detailed replies to emails; time that would be better spent on other tasks.

As a result of this exercise, Peter made changes. He directed colleagues to online company manuals, where they could find answers to their procedural questions. He also kept his email responses brief, and scheduled face-to-face meetings to discuss complicated issues. These two changes freed up 15 hours per month. He was able to begin the special project, and leave work on time most evenings.

If you know or suspect that your time is not being used efficiently, try using the Daily Activity Log for one or two weeks.

DAILY ACTIVITY LOG

Copy this log for each business day over the next one or two weeks. Each day, record your activities in 15-minute increments. If an activity lasts more than 15 minutes, draw an arrow or shade in the total time spent. For example, if you answer emails from 8:00am to 8:45am, write "Answer emails" in the first activity line, and shade in the lines to 8:45am. Rate the priority using the following code: C = Critical (had to be done today); I = Important (specific deadline); L = Low priority (when there is time).

Date: _____

Time	Activity	Priority
8:00am		
8:15		
8:30		
8:45		
9:00		
9:15		
9:30		
9:45		
10:00		
10:15		
10:30		
10:45		
11:00		
11:15		
11:30		
11:45		

✓

12:00pm		
12:15		
12:30		
12:45		
1:00		
1:15		
1:30		
1:45		
2:00		
2:15		
2:30		
2:45		
3:00		
3:15		
3:30		
3:45		
4:00		
4:15		
4:30		
4:45		
5:00		
5:15		
5:30		
5:45		
6:00		

Often, my clients need to improve their efficiency. One of the best ways to do this is by utilizing the expertise of your co-workers. So often, your peers can suggest "hidden" shortcuts, and explain unspoken rules about what is really a priority.

You may also need to change personal habits. Are you adding unnecessary time to projects by striving for perfection? Do you spend long periods trying to solve problems on your own, instead of asking for help? Are you insisting on doing things one way, even though others have suggested shortcuts?

Instead of starting a project from scratch, see if there is an example or template that you can follow. When Janice was charged with writing the company's first customer newsletter, she searched the internet for examples, and then adapted the features to fit her needs.

It is important that you learn how to accurately estimate how long projects will (or should) take. Otherwise, it will be difficult to stay on schedule. One way to make a reasonable estimate is to compare a current project to a similar one from the past. For example, if you once spent 90 minutes to edit 20 pages of a manuscript, it is safe to assume that it will take about the same amount of time to edit 20 pages of an instructional manual. If your current task is more complex, add additional time. An instructional manual that contains 20 pages of text, plus several detailed diagrams, might add 45 minutes to your estimate.

Another way to estimate time is to write down each step of a project, and then make your best guess about how long each step will take. To check the accuracy of your estimate, measure your progress *halfway through* the time you allotted for each step. Suppose you estimated that writing a chapter of an instructional manual would take two hours. After one hour, the chapter should be about 50 percent complete. If it was only 25 percent finished, it would mean that you underestimated the amount of time you needed.

Using this technique of comparing your estimates to the actual amount of time used will help you learn, over time, how to more accurately budget your time.

If you have no idea of what a reasonable time estimate will be, ask your supervisor, your work buddy, or a co-worker for advice: "How much time would you allocate to do X?" or "Does two hours seem like enough time to process all of these orders?"

PLANNING PROJECTS

Here is a basic process that can help you plan and schedule projects:

- Step 1: Write down the task or project, and the completion date.

- Step 2: Break large assignments into smaller steps. Estimate how long it will take you to complete each step. Ask for assistance if you are not sure what all of the steps should be.

- Step 3: Determine what resources you need to complete the project. These can be information, research, materials, equipment, or input from particular individuals. You may need to add additional steps, or more time, to assemble materials or wait for feedback from co-workers.

- Step 4: Schedule when, and for how long, you will work on each step. There might be steps that can be completed in a short period of time, during one day. More complex projects might require several blocks of time, on several different days, for the completion of one step. Work backward from the due date to schedule when you need to complete each step.

  Suppose you need to complete the first chapter of an instruction manual on May 17. The steps to complete the chapter are: creating an outline; writing a draft; and proofreading the final version. To meet the deadline, you decide that you will need to proofread on May 16; complete the draft on May 15; and create the chapter outline on May 13. Your project schedule might look like this:

May 2013

Sun	Mon	Tue	Wed	Thu	Fri	Sat
			1	2	3	4
5	6	7	8	9	10	11
12	13 Create Chapter 1 outline	14	15 Complete draft	16 Proofread	17 Complete Chapter 1	18
19	20	21	22	23	24	25
26	27	28	29	30	31	

If necessary, ask your supervisor to review your schedule. You may need to revise it when something urgent demands your attention.

ⓘ *NT Tip*

Adding extra time into a schedule enables you to deal with unforeseen emergencies, and still complete a project on time.

- Step 5: Set a goal for how much of the entire project should be completed at the halfway point in your schedule.

- Step 6: Monitor your progress by comparing your estimated time to the actual time it takes you to complete each step. This will improve your ability to accurately estimate time. If you allocated two hours to complete a task, and it took you four hours to complete, you either underestimated how much time was necessary, or were not working efficiently.

Steps 5 and 6 are important for learning how to better plan how much time you need, and the pace at which you need to work, to meet deadlines.

- Step 7: When the project is complete, review the results and any areas that need improvement.

The template that follows is an example of how one of my clients used a planning template to schedule the writing of a company manual. The template on pages 98–99 is a blank template that you can download for your own use.

PLANNING TEMPLATE

1. Describe the goal or task: *Produce a process manual*

   Completion date: *1 month*

2. Steps and estimated time to complete:

   Step 1: *Outline sections*

   > Estimated time: *4 hours*

   Step 2: *Identify colleagues who will edit each section*

   > Estimated time: *1 hour*

   Step 3: *Write first draft*

   > Estimated time: *40 hours (4 hours per day, 5 days per week for 2 weeks)*

   Step 4: *Send draft to colleagues for editing*

   > Estimated time: *30 minutes to send and 1 week for comments*

   Step 5: *Incorporate feedback into final document*

   > Estimated time: *2 hours*

   Total estimated time: *47½ hours plus 1 week for comments*

3. What I need to complete the task (materials, information, equipment, etc.): *Samples of process documents from other departments, organizational chart, meeting with supervisor to review initial outline*

4. I will work on this project from: *9:30–11:30am and 3:30–5:30pm on Mondays, Wednesdays and Thursdays; 11:00am–1:00pm and 4:00–6:00pm on Tuesdays and 8:30am–12:30pm on Fridays*

5. At the halfway point, my goal is to have the following amount of work completed: *60 percent of the first draft written*

6. *Actual* time to complete:

Step 1: *3½ hours*

Step 2: *45 minutes*

Step 3: *60 hours*

Step 4: *15 minutes/2 weeks for all comments*

Step 5: *6 hours*

Total actual time: *70½ hours and 1 extra week for comments*

7. If the actual time to complete a step/task took longer than the estimated time:

a) What obstacles, if any, were not anticipated? *Draft took much longer due to unfamiliarity with part of the product development process; colleagues had more changes than I expected; two managers could not get feedback to me within a week due to travel schedules.*

b) How can the task be handled differently next time? *Allow 50 percent more time to write the document than I expect; check managers' travel schedules in advance; make sure that I am familiar with all aspects of the development process before beginning project.*

✓

PLANNING TEMPLATE

Readers have permission to download this template for personal use, from www.jkp.com/catalogue/book/9781849059435/resources.

1. Describe the goal or task: _____

   Completion date: _____

2. Steps and estimated time to complete:

   Step 1: _____

       Estimated time: _____

   Step 2: _____

       Estimated time: _____

   Step 3: _____

       Estimated time: _____

   Step 4: _____

       Estimated time: _____

   Step 5: _____

       Estimated time: _____

   Total estimated time: _____

3. What I need to complete the task (materials, information, equipment, etc.): _____

4. I will work on this project from: _____

   _____

5. At the halfway point, my goal is to have the following amount of work completed: _____

6. *Actual* time to complete:

   Step 1: _____

   Step 2: _____

   Step 3: _____

Step 4: _____

Step 5: _____

Total actual time: _____

7. If the actual time to complete a step/task took longer than the estimated time:

a) What obstacles, if any, were not anticipated? _____

_____

_____

b) How can the task be handled differently next time? _____

_____

_____

GETTING TO THE POINT: RIGHT-SIZING COMMUNICATIONS

"My biggest challenge is concise communication, both written and verbal," said John. "I have been repeatedly criticized, even mocked, that I make things too wordy." John explained that he included a lot of detail to make sure that people completely understood what he meant. Ironically, the opposite happened. People were confused by his long, tangential missives and discussions. They stopped reading his epic emails and tuned him out during meetings.

Providing your colleagues with the information they need, in a way that they can easily access and use it, is a vital workplace skill. Individuals who have trouble communicating clearly may be perceived as unprofessional or disorganized. At one company, an employee who sent multiple, long emails was seen as disrespectful of other people's time.

There are several reasons why individuals overcommunicate, such as:

- difficulty organizing one's thoughts and planning the purpose of the communication

- inability to separate relevant from irrelevant data

- not matching content to the needs, knowledge base and expectations of the audience

- little awareness of time, and how long they have been talking, or how long it will take a recipient to read a document.

It is also possible to be too concise. You will know this if your colleagues frequently ask you to elaborate on your ideas, or provide more information.

Here are some tips about how to make your workplace communication more effective:

- *Plan your message.* Whenever possible, decide specifically what information you need to convey before you start writing or speaking. Prepare an outline with key points, and ask a colleague to review it. Think about what is really important. Jim included many irrelevant details that made it hard for co-workers to understand his main message: "Yesterday, at 11:38am during the conference call…" He also spelled out the obvious: "Created a budget that includes costs for editing, formatting, printing and mailing the newsletter." Jim's colleagues did not need to know at what time a topic was discussed.

They were all aware that the budget included costs for producing the various elements of a newsletter.

Before you include a detail, complete this sentence: "This is important to my audience because…"

Challenge yourself to communicate the main points using 25 words or less.

Read meeting agendas in advance and stick to the topics that are listed. If you plan to contribute to a topic, prepare bullet points in advance to keep yourself focused. If there is no formal agenda, think about the purpose of the meeting, and do not bring up unrelated subjects.

- *Think audience and context.* In order to decide which details are important, you must understand the knowledge base, needs and expectations of your audience (even if that audience is only one other person).

Are you communicating with subordinates, peers, a supervisor, senior management, or outside parties such as customers or vendors? What do they already know about the situation? What do they need to know now? A customer complaining about a late shipment wants a delivery date, not a long story about why a package was delayed. Senior managers are interested in strategy and results, not the steps of launching a marketing campaign.

At meetings, notice the other people who are present. Who talks, about what, and for how long? Silently scan the room and notice people's body language. Do they seem interested, excited, concerned, bored or confused? When people are shifting in their chairs, glancing at their watches, focusing on their handheld devices, or staring out the window, they're bored, and want to end the meeting or move on to another speaker or subject.

If noticing and interpreting body language is difficult for you, arrange for a colleague you trust, your work buddy, or your supervisor, to signal you when it is time to stop speaking.

Pay attention to the length and content of emails that you receive from co-workers. Are your missives longer, shorter or similar?

More Thoughts about Email

Email has specific benefits for people with Asperger's Syndrome. You can usually take your time creating or replying to a message. There are no worries about making eye contact, or being caught off guard by a question you can't answer.

Unfortunately, the very things that make email attractive also make it notorious for creating misunderstandings. Innocent remarks can be perceived as threats, and attempts at humor can be interpreted as insults. The annals of the corporate world are filled with stories about angry or inflammatory emails that got their authors fired. Sometimes, people discover that they have spent the better part of an afternoon crafting lengthy replies about subjects that can't be resolved in cyberspace. If several people receive the email, your inbox can rapidly fill with dozens of missives to read and reply to. Many of your responses will be out of date by the time you hit the Send button.

Email can be an effective tool for conveying basic information and answering straightforward questions. Keep the messages brief. If your emails frequently exceed half of a printed page, or you are sending more than three about the same topic, email is probably not the best medium.

Unless the matter is urgent, wait 48 hours before you send an email asking whether the recipient has read your previous message.

- *Avoid "$20 words."* His co-workers also complained that John used *$20 words.* This expression refers to words that are unusual, too formal, or that may not be understood by a person who does not have a large vocabulary. Several years ago, I coached a young man who was concerned about "bloviating" during job interviews. *Bloviate* is a word which is not often used; it means verbose and/or pompous. Continual use of obscure or unusual words can make you seem pretentious, aloof, or insecure, and may intimidate others.

- *Edit your written communication.* Whenever possible, set a written document aside for at least an hour, and preferably overnight. Reading it with a fresh eye will probably reveal words, phrases, or points that can be cut. Read your words out loud to notice whether there are extra words or run-on sentences. Many people find it easier to edit their work by printing out a copy, instead of looking at a computer screen.

- *Choose the right medium for the message.* You may feel very comfortable with email, however, some situations are best handled with a telephone call or face-to-face meeting. Many people are overwhelmed by the number of emails they receive each day. They will not have time to read long, involved messages. Complex situations, big decisions, and sensitive topics are not appropriate to address via email.

BEING FLEXIBLE AND SEEING OPTIONS

A flexible mindset allows you to adapt to changing circumstances and make better decisions. Neurotypicals are skilled at approaching problems from different perspectives, identifying options, and making decisions about the best option to choose. People with Asperger's Syndrome have a tendency to be rigid in their thinking, and less able to see the various choices that are available.

Sometimes, clients become angry when I ask them to brainstorm options with me. They insist that their solution is the only one. Invariably, after a few minutes of looking for alternatives, a list of choices is created. There are always *at least* two options for responding to any situation. Accepting this gives you power. It is frightening and depressing to believe that there is only one way.

The reality is that conditions are always changing, sometimes for the better and sometimes for the worse. Company policies change. New managers arrive, and with them, new expectations. Technology, regulations and economic events transform industries. Companies go out of business, merge with other organizations, or reorganize and lay off workers.

Lynn was exhausted and burned out after months of working 10–12-hour days. "I feel like I am disintegrating," she said, as she described her difficulty sleeping, fatigue, and the growing list of errands and household chores that weren't getting done.

When I suggested that we list her options, Lynn exclaimed, "I don't *have* any! We're understaffed at work, there is a hiring freeze, and I just can't get everything done."

I decided to start things off. "Well, you could quit."

"But I need my paycheck," Lynn replied.

"Okay. Option number one won't work. What about looking for a job at a different company?"

"I just don't have the energy," she said. "I don't even have an up-to-date resume."

"So option number two isn't feasible, either. What else could you do?" I asked.

Now that Lynn was more relaxed, she could think more clearly. "If I could just get some time to concentrate, without any interruptions, I could get a lot more done."

Progress!

Lynn and I talked about how she could implement this option, and came up with several ideas: take a laptop into an empty conference room; work from home; place a Do Not Disturb sign on the entrance to her cubicle; send all of her calls to voicemail; close her email program. All of these would provide some uninterrupted work time.

"These might work in the short term," Lynn said, "but my boss says that I take too long on projects, and create extra work for myself. I don't know how to streamline my process."

"Let's keep brainstorming," I suggested.

Once again, Lynn was becoming agitated. She began explaining why her situation was hopeless.

"Another option is that you can do nothing, and just accept things as they are," I ventured.

Lynn looked at me in surprise.

"Choosing to do nothing won't improve things," I explained, "but *is* an option."

After a few seconds, Lynn said, "I could ask Dean, one of my co-workers, how he manages the workload."

This made a total of five different options. Not all of them were possible or desirable. However, creating periods of uninterrupted work time, and getting suggestions from a co-worker had the potential to reduce Lynn's stress and the length of her work days.

Flexibility is also a factor in good decision-making. Choosing the best way to react to a situation is rarely dependent on just one detail. It depends on the context within which something is happening, and the other people involved, as Sandra discovered.

As production manager for a specialty publisher, Sandra formats editorial copy, positions advertisements, oversees the printing of magazines and newsletters, and makes sure that publications are mailed to subscribers on time. At her last performance review, she was praised for her meticulous attention to detail and perfect on-time production record.

One Monday afternoon, David, the managing editor, informed Sandra that a feature article for the company's flagship publication would be late. It was being rewritten to include breaking industry news. Sandra would not receive editorial copy on Tuesday morning as expected. David wasn't exactly sure when she would get the final manuscript. "It will definitely be by the end of the week," he assured her.

This meant that Sandra would not be able to give a final layout to Ed, the editor-in-chief, on Friday morning.

"David *knows* the deadlines, and that Ed has to sign off on the final layout," Sandra exclaimed. "When I asked David to review the production schedule, he said no, and that the rewrites were in the best interest of the readers. He told me I had to be flexible and figure out how to make up the lost time. How is sending the magazine out late in the best interest of readers?!"

Focusing exclusively on the production schedule caused Sandra to miss the bigger picture, and adapt to the change in plans. David's job was to ensure a quality editorial product. He knew that breaking news took precedence over meeting production deadlines. Sandra didn't look at the situation from David's perspective. To her, David's comments about being flexible were puzzling.

"What option do I have but to miss the deadline?" she asked. "David doesn't care about deadlines, so the magazine will be late, and I will be blamed because other people are not following the rules."

Here are the steps we used to understand the situation in a different way:

- Step 1: View the facts objectively and unemotionally.

- Step 2: Analyze why something is happening; does it make sense?

- Step 3: Compare to a previous, similar situation.

- Step 4: Brainstorm options.

When Sandra learned that David's article would be late, she reacted emotionally, with fear about missing a deadline. Paralyzed by the emotional turmoil, she began to cry in her office.

An objective review of the facts put the situation into a different light. Breaking news would be of interest to readers, and for this reason, David decided that they wouldn't be upset if the magazine arrived a few days late.

"It makes sense to me that David wants to rewrite the article," Sandra said.

She then thought back to a previous job that she had at a newspaper. "Stories were late all the time," she said, "My boss used to build extra days into the production schedule because of it." Then she smiled, "I can do the same thing!"

We also brainstormed options that Sandra had with the production schedule. One of the options was to check with the printer to see if the schedule could be adjusted. The printer said yes, which meant that the issue would be only two days late.

Once she understood how David's decision made sense, Sandra realized why he asked her to be flexible with the schedule. Doing so is what is expected of a proactive production manager. Sandra's willingness to accommodate the editorial change made her a more valuable member of the organization, and demonstrated that she was a team player.

The process of objective analysis and brainstorming options is one way to be a more flexible problem-solver. Another way is to practice grayscale thinking. I notice that people with Asperger's Syndrome tend to think in absolute terms: something is good or bad; right or wrong. Grayscale thinking allows for choices: doing X *and* Y; developing "if/then" scenarios. Instead of working all afternoon on one project, and not responding to any calls or emails, a grayscale thinker would do both: work for a period of time on the project, *and* spend time replying to voicemails and emails.

Challenge yourself to come up with a minimum of three options to solve any problem or situation you encounter. Whenever possible, brainstorm with someone else, so that you generate even more possibilities. Write down all of the ideas without judging their feasibility. When you are finished brainstorming, examine each idea and its likely outcome, and decide which to eliminate and which to implement.

Another way to develop mental flexibility is to practice the debater's trick of arguing the opposing view. Take an idea that you disagree with, and then find the merit in it.

SETTING REALISTIC GOALS

Whether you want to improve your job performance, get along better with co-workers, or find a new career, it is important that you set a clear goal. Many of my clients set goals that are vague, too general, or difficult to act upon: "Get along better with others" or "Be more efficient."

The SMART goals template enables you to define your goal, create benchmarks to measure your progress, and determine whether your goal is realistic. SMART is an acronym that stands for **S**pecific, **M**easurable, **A**chievable, **R**easonable, and **T**ime-oriented. There are five steps to creating a SMART goal:

- Step 1: Make the goal **S**pecific.

- Step 2: Make success **M**easurable.

- Step 3: Select a goal that you can **A**chieve.

- Step 4: Check that your goal is **R**easonable.

- Step 5: Make it **T**ime-oriented.

Seth is a journal editor who was introduced in Chapter 3, in the section about meeting employer expectations. This is an example of how Seth used the SMART technique to address his problem managing his new production duties.

- Step 1: Specific goal: *Produce editions of the journal on time and without errors, beginning with the fall issue.*

  Originally, Seth's objective was to "avoid production problems," which is general and hard to quantify. His new goal is specific and actionable.

- Step 2: Measurement of success: *Issues will be laid out correctly the first time, and I will avoid having to fix mistakes at the last minute.*

  This step defines how you will know that you have reached your goal.

- Step 3: Verify that the goal is achievable: *Yes, with the use of detailed checklists and training from a knowledgeable staff member.*

  This step is a "reality check." Do you have the skills, ability and resources to meet your objective?

  If you realize at this stage that you have set an unachievable goal, do not despair. You might need to take an intermediate step first, such as acquiring a particular skill. Or, you might need to go back to step one and adjust your goal.

- Step 4: Goal is reasonable: *Even with training, I cannot rely only on my memory to get everything done. Using a checklist is a realistic way to make sure that I do not forget a step.*

   Steps 3 and 4 sound similar, but there is a difference. Step 3 verifies that you have set a goal that is possible to achieve. Step 4 verifies that it is realistic given your circumstances. For instance, while it is *possible* that Seth could remember all of the steps after some training, relying on his memory is not *realistic*. Unrealistic goals lead to frustration.

- Step 5: Goal is time-oriented: *The fall issue will be produced on time and without errors.*

   Setting a (reasonable!) time frame for reaching a goal helps you stay focused and motivated. Establishing an end date allows you to work backward and create a timeline for taking various actions. It also helps you plan interim benchmarks to monitor your progress.

Monitoring your progress and adjusting your plan are integral to reaching goals (Meltzer 2007). If you notice that one strategy isn't working, do not continue it. Try something different instead.

If your goal will take several months or more to attain, interim goals will provide a sense of accomplishment and help you stay motivated. Try setting immediate goals: achievable within the next two weeks; mid-range goals: achievable within the next two to three months; and a long-term goal: achievable in six months or more.

On the next page is a SMART goals planning template that you can use to set realistic goals.

✓

SMART GOALS PLANNER

SMART is an acronym for Specific, Measurable, Achievable, Reasonable, and Time-oriented. This model helps you develop realistic goals and a step-by-step plan to reach them.

Step 1: Specific goal (What do you want, by when?):_____

_____

_____

Step 2: Measure of success (How will you know when you've achieved the goal?): _____

_____

_____

Step 3: Achievable (Do you have the skills, ability and resources needed to meet your objective? If you answer "no," what skills/resources do you need to acquire? Do you need to modify your goal?): _____

_____

_____

Step 4: Reality check: Is the goal reasonable? (Are you willing to put in time and effort over a realistic time frame?): _____

_____

_____

Step 5: Time-oriented (When do you want to achieve your goal? Use this date to work backward and create an action step timeline): _____

_____

_____

CREATING AN ACTION PLAN THAT WORKS

Setting a goal doesn't mean much if you are not able to follow through with effective action. Are any of these "action inhibitors" getting in your way?

- Unsure of how to begin or what the specific steps are.

- Anxiety about a particular step (e.g. afraid of making phone calls).

- Boredom with tasks.

- Negative thinking: "It won't work anyway, so why bother?"

- Distraction: spend hours surfing the internet, instead of taking action toward a goal.

- Action items are not scheduled: forget what to do.

- Trying to make a change with little or no support.

- Action items are too large or too general.

An action plan establishes the specific steps you will take, and when, to reach your goal. Consistent action, over a reasonable period of time, gets results. Sometimes people are concerned that if they are not making huge strides toward their goals every week, they will not be successful. I have found the opposite to be true: small steps, executed consistently, get big and better results.

Your chance of success is higher if your goal is meaningful and important to *you*. Todd learned at his performance review that he did not engage enough with colleagues, and would not receive the promotion that he wanted. This motivated him to work on his interpersonal communication skills.

Even if the fear of losing your job is your primary motivator, try to find a positive reason for making a change.

Planning action steps on a weekly basis keeps the process manageable. Commit only to actions that you will do. If you look at your plan and feel anxious or overwhelmed, you need to make revisions. Below is a simple template for planning weekly action items.

✓

WEEKLY GOALS AND ACTION ITEMS

For the week of:_____

GOALS FOR THIS WEEK

1. _____

   Specific steps I will take toward this goal:

   a) _____

   b) _____

   c) _____

   d) _____

2. _____

   Specific steps I will take toward this goal:

   a) _____

   b) _____

   c) _____

   d) _____

3. _____

   Specific steps I will take toward this goal:

   a) _____

   b) _____

   c) _____

   d) _____

✓

PROGRESS

Goal	Action Steps Achieved?	Results
1	☐ Yes ☐ No	
2	☐ Yes ☐ No	
3	☐ Yes ☐ No	

My level of satisfaction with my progress this week:

☐ Very satisfied

☐ Somewhat satisfied

☐ Not satisfied

Making yourself accountable to another person will help you stay motivated. Arrange regular, frequent check-ins with your coach, mentor, counselor, co-worker, or family member. Tell this person beforehand what he should do if you do not follow through with your commitments.

If you try something and it doesn't work, it simply means that you need to find a different approach. Too often, people allow one or two setbacks to completely stop their progress. It is not realistic to expect that everything you try will work, or produce immediate results. My most successful clients are the ones who take small, consistent steps, and are willing to experiment.

> ⓘ *NT Tip*
> One of my favorite action strategies is the three-item to do list described in *Find Your Focus Zone* (Palladino 2007, pp.144–5). Select three things to do, and focus on these only. When they are done, move on to the next three, and then the next three, etc.

Having a hard time getting started? Then force yourself to begin…one thing …*now*! Once you begin an activity, the doing is usually not that difficult. Action begets more action, and most people find that they can work longer and more productively than they initially thought possible.

Set a timer for 15 minutes, and focus on a task until the timer goes off. Review your progress, and decide whether to continue working, or move on to something else.

Some people complete easy tasks first, because the sense of accomplishment motivates them to keep working. Others do the opposite: they start with demanding tasks, when their energy level is higher, and then "relax" by doing easier ones (Palladino 2007). Experiment and see which way works best for you.

This action plan was created by James. He wanted to find a similar job with a different company. James worried that his skills were out of date, and that he would not be able to make as much money at another firm.

Action Item: Research the salary range and skill requirements for senior software programmers.

Steps:

- Search online job boards for open positions (Monday, 7:00–8:00pm)

    Create spreadsheet of requirements (programming languages, types of projects, years of experience)

- Join one or two online groups for programmers (Monday, 7:00–8:00pm)

    Is salary addressed on message boards?

- Visit website of local programmer's professional association (Wednesday, 7:30–8:00pm)

    Salary surveys? Price of membership?

- Create a profile on LinkedIn (Saturday, 10:00–11:00am)

    Invite at least three colleagues to connect during the next week

- Visit at least two salary-survey websites (Sunday, 9:30–10:00am)

Notice how manageable the steps are. James assigned himself specific dates and times to complete each task. As he worked through his action items, he realized that he had been making a lot of guesses and assumptions that weren't true. He was delighted to discover that there were many high-paying jobs that he was qualified to perform.

ⓘ *NT Tip*

Maintain your motivation by rewarding yourself with something meaningful. The reward doesn't have to cost money. Nancy de-cluttered her office in 15-minute intervals, three days per week. After each interval, she rewarded herself with ten minutes of internet surfing time.

CHAPTER 6

MANAGING ANGER, FRUSTRATION, ANXIETY, AND STRESS

"I have no concept of 'checking in' or recognizing my own emotions... and therefore may keep going until anxiety, anger or stress has built up significantly." (Inventory Control Specialist, age 32)

John became so frustrated with a co-worker that he "lost it," and quit his job on the spot. With great effort, he was able to convince his employer to rehire him, but the damage was done. "After nearly a decade with this company, my role has been reduced," John said, "and I am no longer invited to the strategy meetings."

Elizabeth was so anxious about a missed deadline that she exploded at a colleague for calling her "Beth." Ellen abruptly walked out of a department meeting because she could not follow the rapid pace of the discussion. Bill began cursing when his boss wouldn't stop "barraging" him with questions about a troubled project...and was promptly fired for insubordination.

It is extremely important that you control your emotions, especially anger, in the workplace. People will not want to work with you if you act in ways that are frightening or offensive. If you say or do something that others perceive as a threat, to their person or company property, you will be fired and possibly arrested.

Even if you don't lose your job, you will lose your credibility. Others may question your emotional stability, maturity or judgment. You might earn a reputation for being unreasonable. Once a relationship with your supervisor or co-workers is damaged, it is very hard to repair. Disclosing that you have Asperger's Syndrome and trouble managing your emotions is not an excuse.

These behaviors will damage your reputation and possibly get you fired:

- losing your temper: yelling, cursing, slamming your hand on a desk or a wall, throwing objects

- crying frequently or hysterically, especially over minor incidents

- withdrawing and refusing to answer questions

- abruptly walking out of meetings

- making dramatic accusations of being "tortured," "persecuted," or "hated by everyone"

- muttering under your breath

- threatening to harm yourself, another person, or company property.

Emotional "meltdowns" are activated by the brain. When a person perceives danger, whether real or imagined, the brain responds through two pathways. One is conscious and rational, the other is unconscious and instinctive (Johnson 2003). The emotional memory of a threat is stored in the brain, where the amygdala triggers an immediate, instinctual response (Goleman 1998).

This response can override the rational part of the brain, so that a person reacts without thinking. This is useful during a true emergency, when there isn't time to methodically think a situation through, and develop a plan of action. However, when the small, daily frustrations and stresses of life cause a person to lose control, the individual is experiencing an "amygdala hijack" (Goleman 1998, p.74). This term was coined by Daniel Goleman to describe strong, automatic emotional reactions, particularly fear and anger, that are out of proportion to the situation.

There is evidence that a faulty amygdala may be to blame for the characteristic difficulty that people with Asperger's Syndrome have with managing their emotions, particularly anger. In *The Complete Guide to Asperger's Syndrome*, Tony Attwood discusses research revealing structural and functional differences in the amygdala in individuals who are on the autism spectrum (Attwood 2007). This may explain the decreased awareness of one's emotional state. Most neurotypicals are able to notice and monitor rising levels of frustration and anger. People with Asperger's Syndrome tend to go from calm to the point of losing control in one step (Attwood 2007). Attwood explains:

> …the amygdala can be structurally and functionally abnormal in children and adults with Asperger's syndrome. The amygdala has many functions, including perception and regulation of emotions, especially fear and anger… The amygdala functions as the dashboard of [a] car, providing

the driver with warning signals regarding the temperature of the engine, the amount of oil and fuel, and speed of the vehicle. In the case of people with Asperger's syndrome, the "dashboard" is not functioning consistently. Information on the increasing emotional "heat" and functioning of the engine (emotion and stress levels) are not available to the driver as a warning of impending breakdown. (Attwood 2007, p.145)

Many clients tell me that stress makes them more prone to "meltdowns." Indeed, stress hormones can build up in the body, to the point that an insignificant event will trigger an amygdala hijack (Goleman 1998).

It is my experience that simply trying to function in the neurotypical world is a significant stressor for a person with Asperger's Syndrome. This is why it is important to find ways to manage the levels of stress in your life, so that small events won't trigger inappropriate emotional reactions. If you have a serious difficulty controlling your emotions, especially anger, seek assistance from a qualified clinician. Otherwise, consider implementing one or more of the following suggestions for coping with stress.

Learn what triggers your anger, frustration, anxiety or panic. I ask my clients to make notes of their triggers over a one or two-week period. Then, we look for patterns, and strategize how to interrupt the automatic, undesirable reactions.

One of Erin's triggers was being interrupted while she was trying to prepare week-end sales reports. She would snap at co-workers who asked her questions, and then have trouble refocusing on the task. Erin began updating the reports on a laptop that she set up in an empty conference room.

Josh realized that he became irritated by people and events in general, during the late afternoon. His trigger was hunger, brought on by Josh's habit of skipping lunch. He now brings lunch to his workplace each day and makes sure to eat.

In addition to noticing what triggers an emotional response, learn to recognize the signals your body sends as your emotions become more and more intense. This will help you avoid an outburst. You might notice that moderate irritation causes your shoulder muscles to become tense. When you are very irritated, you might notice a pounding in your temples, and clenching of your fists and jaw.

John's reputation for being "explosive" had cost him a promotion. His colleagues in the engineering group were tired of his angry responses to their questions. They considered John to be disrespectful and mean.

It soon became clear to John that feeling pressured to come up with immediate answers to complex questions triggered his anger. He could actually feel his stomach muscles tighten, and his throat become dry.

John has changed the way that he interacted with his colleagues. Since fatigue makes him less patient, whenever possible he avoids discussing complicated projects late in the afternoon. When he notices his stomach tightening, he knows that the question is one that he needs to think about. He says, "Let me think about the situation and get back you."

Noticing triggers and levels of emotional arousal will help you "short-circuit" an amygdala hijack by keeping your stress levels under control. Here are suggestions for managing stress:

- *Take a break.* The act of physically leaving a stressful environment can restore emotional calm, and rational thinking. Get a drink of water, walk around the parking lot, or listen to music on your iPod.

- *Excuse yourself from the discussion.* You can say: "I need some time to think; let's talk again tomorrow" or "I am upset right now, and want to calm down before discussing this further."

- *Practice positive self-talk.* Create a repertoire of empowering statements that you can repeat silently to yourself during stressful moments: "I can handle this situation" or "If I approach the problem calmly, the answer will come to me."

- *Exercise regularly.* It is a proven stress reducer that also improves your mood and general health. Many individuals on the autism spectrum report positive benefits from yoga.

- *Meditate.* This is another proven method for restoring calm. There are many books that describe various meditation techniques. You can also find instruction at adult education programs and yoga centers.

- *Get enough sleep.* Many, many clients tell me that a good night's sleep makes them more patient and less reactive. Well-rested people are better decision-makers, too. If getting enough sleep is a chronic problem, consult a medical professional.

- *Schedule time for your special interest.* Individuals with Asperger's Syndrome consistently report that engaging in their favorite activity is an emotional restorative.

- *Accept that things will not always go the way that you would like.* Holding a job requires flexibility, and a willingness to compromise. It is not possible to control the actions of other people. However, you can control the way that *you* respond, and how others perceive you.

PUT THE ACTIONS OF OTHERS INTO PERSPECTIVE

It is a given that you will encounter people at work who annoy, frustrate, or otherwise provoke you. I have noticed that people with Asperger's Syndrome frequently take the actions of other people very personally. Completely innocent remarks are interpreted as attacks or put-downs.

On his first day, Tim's supervisor came to his cubicle to begin training him on the order entry process. Tim turned on the computer, and the two sat waiting for it to boot up. After a few minutes, Tim's supervisor said, "It usually doesn't take this long to get started."

Tim thought that he was being accused of damaging the computer.

"It sounds to me like your supervisor was stating her concern that something might be wrong with the computer," I said.

Tim thought about it, and replied, "You're right. I always assume that people think problems are my fault."

Sharon was close to tears at the beginning of our coaching session. "Bill doesn't like me," she said, "otherwise why would he make me look bad to the head of the division?"

Bill was Sharon's supervisor. When he had promoted Sharon the previous month, he offered her a larger cubicle that was very close to his office. Sharon asked for some time to think about it. She didn't like change, and was concerned that the new cubicle would put her within earshot of a co-worker with whom there had been conflicts.

Four weeks later, Sharon was upset with Bill. "When the head of our division asked Bill why I wasn't in a bigger cubicle, Bill told him that I don't want to move," Sharon said. "That's a lie! I never said that, and now the division vice president will think that I am ungrateful."

It was puzzling to me that Sharon thought that Bill disliked her, particularly since he had just given her a promotion. Sharon described how, several months earlier, Bill had eliminated funds for freelance help from Sharon's budget. There were no cuts to the budget for freelance graphic designers. To Sharon, this meant that Bill liked the art director better. Now, she worried that Bill wanted to make her look bad to the vice president.

We discussed Sharon's pattern of interpreting the actions of co-workers as personal affronts, and her tendency to presume the worst in any situation.

"It sounds to me like the budget cut was a business decision," I said. "At that time, you mentioned that there were company-wide layoffs."

I also offered a different take on the cubicle situation. A larger workspace, in closer proximity to a senior staff member, is considered a perk. It communicated Sharon's higher rank within the company. Bill was so sure that Sharon would be excited about the bigger space, that he had already told the vice president about the change. As the weeks went on and Sharon continued to ruminate about whether to relocate, Bill concluded that she didn't want the bigger cubicle. When the vice president casually asked why Sharon hadn't moved, Bill was simply answering his question.

Taking things personally is an example of a *cognitive distortion*. This is a habitual pattern of negative thinking that results in misreading people and situations. Thoughts associated with cognitive distortions are automatically negative. Something happens, you immediately form a conclusion about why, and don't stop to consider whether the conclusion makes sense. *The big tip-off that your perceptions are distorted is the lack of evidence to support them.*

The concept of cognitive distortion was introduced by Dr. David Burns, a pioneer in the field of cognitive therapy. He demonstrated that people can lessen feelings of anxiety, depression, and other negative emotions by changing the way they think about the events in their lives. These are the ten common patterns of distorted thinking that Burns identified in *Feeling Good: The New Mood Therapy* (Burns 1980, pp.42–3). Do you recognize any of these patterns in *your* thinking?

1. *Polarized (all or nothing) thinking*: seeing people and situations in absolute terms, such as good or bad, right or wrong, smart or stupid.

2. *Catastrophizing*: the tendency to exaggerate the potential for negative outcomes. Your boss points out one error in an assignment, and you decide that he's getting ready to fire you.

3. *"Shoulds"*: a strict set of rules about how people, including yourself, are supposed to act or do things, with exaggerated consequences if a rule is violated. Ellen thinks that colleagues should always meet deadlines, or be fired.

4. *Personalization*: assuming that you are the reason that someone behaved in a certain way, without considering other explanations: "Todd didn't say hello to me because he doesn't like me."

5. *Jumping to conclusions*: *mind reading*, where you conclude that someone is reacting negatively to you, without any evidence that this is true: "Dan didn't fix my computer because he wants my projects to be late;" or *fortune telling*, which is anticipating what could go wrong as an established fact: "The project will fail and I'll lose my job."

6. *Labeling*: assigning negative labels to yourself or other people without having evidence to support that conclusion: "My co-workers are selfish and unsupportive because they wouldn't cover for me" or "The division head is an idiot for not giving me the promotion."

7. *Filtering*: paying attention only to negative information and filtering out positive information. Jill obsessed over one "needs improvement" in her performance review, and ignored the overall rating of "exceeds expectations" and the recommendation that she receive a raise.

8. *Disqualifying positives*: insisting that positive experiences don't count: "Anyone could have received the award."

9. *Emotional reasoning*: the belief that your *feelings* are the truth: "I feel stupid, so I must *be* stupid" or "I'm worried about losing my job, so they must be ready to fire me."

10. *Overgeneralization*: global statements about one-time events. Because you entered one wrong formula into a spreadsheet, you believe that you're no good at budgeting. Or, you get off at the wrong subway stop and believe that you cannot use public transportation.

Cognitive distortions are not unique to individuals with Asperger's Syndrome. However, the characteristic anxiety, and difficulty interpreting nonverbal cues, understanding another person's perspective, and grasping situational context make cognitive distortions more likely. Depression also predisposes someone toward a negative outlook.

HOW TO CHANGE DISTORTED THINKING PATTERNS

Distorted thinking patterns originate with the *thought* you have about an event, not the event itself. Your thought causes you to feel a certain way, and you react based on that feeling.

Mark's supervisor pointed out three typographical errors in his article, and asked Mark to proofread more carefully. Mark thought that his supervisor was questioning his ability as a writer. This thought made Mark angry, and he accused his supervisor of picking on him. Had Mark interpreted the feedback as helpful advice about how to make his writing more professional, he would have reacted in a positive way.

Whenever negative thinking prevents the logical, objective analysis of a situation, the conclusions you draw or assumptions you make are suspect.

It is not easy to change negative thinking patterns. However, it is worth the effort if a negative outlook is interfering with your ability to get along with other people, or achieve your goals.

Begin by connecting your thoughts to the behavior that you want to change. Allison wanted to find a different job for over two years. Each time she tried to update her resume, she became paralyzed. I asked her to write down the thoughts that went through her mind when she started the update.

Allison realized that looking at her resume brought up thoughts about an unsuccessful job search from five years ago. She *over-generalized* that one experience to mean that, "I'm no good at interviewing, so I can't find another job."

Next, challenge your negative thought and replace it with one that is more realistic *and that you believe is true*. Take your time with this step. The new thought you choose must be one that you really believe is true, or this process won't work. Allison created a new belief about job seeking: "When I learn better interviewing skills, I will communicate my capabilities and be offered a job."

The Rationality of Beliefs Checklist is a tool that you can use to test the validity of your current thought patterns. It is printed here with the kind permission of Dr. Lewis Stern.

RATIONALITY OF BELIEFS CHECKLIST

When you would like to make sure that specific beliefs you hold or assumptions you have are rational, there are some check-points to help. The following questions can help you explore whether your beliefs or assumptions make sense, and fit with reality and with what others you respect would think.

For any belief or assumption you want to check for rationality, begin by writing it down. Then answer each of the following ten questions about that belief or assumption. For each question you answer *yes*, you get one point. When you are done answering the questions, tally your points to see how many of them you get out of ten. The more times you tick *yes*, the more likely it is that your belief or assumption is rational. The more times you tick *no*, the more you may want to consider alternative beliefs or assumptions that could help you be more successful, happy, and comfortable with your decisions and actions, and reduce your level of negative stress.

Yes No

☐ ☐ 1. Are you comfortable with the possibility that you may be wrong?

☐ ☐ 2. Is this belief/assumption based on an objective view of the facts and does it fit with other relevant facts that you know to be true?

☐ ☐ 3. Consider what would happen in the future as a consequence of this belief/assumption. How likely is it that this will actually happen?

☐ ☐ 4. Does believing this help protect your life and health?

☐ ☐ 5. Do you *never* deny, exaggerate, or avoid facts or events which may show this to be wrong?

☐ ☐ 6. Does this belief/assumption coincide with what you have been told by other people who are usually rational?

☐ ☐ 7. Does believing this help you achieve your short- and long-range goals?

☐   ☐   8. When you hear or think of opposing views are you open-minded and really willing to consider that they may be true and you may be wrong?

☐   ☐   9. Does believing this help you prevent useless conflict with other people?

☐   ☐   10. Does believing this help you feel the way that you need and want to?

1 point for each *yes*

Total: _____ points.

It takes practice to reinforce a new thought pattern. Allison wrote her new belief on pieces of paper, and placed them where she would see them several times each day. She read books about effective interviewing techniques. We began role playing interview scenarios in our coaching sessions. Over the course of several weeks, Allison's confidence improved and she was able to update her resume.

Here are some ideas for helping a new thought take root:

- Set a goal based on the new thought pattern, and start taking action.

- Focus on positive outcomes associated with the new thought.

- Repeat the thought silently to yourself, as an affirmation, multiple times each day.

- Write the thought on sticky notes and post them in areas where you will see them often.

MANAGING ANXIETY

"I am constantly under a low level of stress, always on the lookout for 'something' to occur, some undefined vague threat. I'm always on guard." (IT Consultant, age 49)

I remember attending a conference for adults with Asperger's Syndrome. The speaker asked the audience: how many had problems with anxiety in their lives? In the audience of over 100, every single hand went up!

Every human being experiences anxiety. In the right amount, it can be a source of motivation. Concern about an up-coming performance review can provide the impetus to work on interpersonal communication skills.

Anxiety is often a response to thoughts about what *might* happen in the future. This is different from fear, which is a reaction to an actual threatening event. Common triggers of anxiety include:

- performing a task for the first time, especially if the steps aren't clear

- recalling a previous bad experience with the same or similar task/ situation

- concern about making a mistake

- fear of being criticized or ridiculed by others.

Anxiety is a common feature among individuals with Asperger's Syndrome (Attwood 2007). For some, it becomes a chronic state. I notice certain anxiety triggers that are common to my clients with Asperger's Syndrome. They include:

- not doing something perfectly

- speaking to people you don't know (in person or on the telephone)

- not knowing what to say

- anticipating a negative outcome

- being pressured to make quick decisions

- making decisions, in general

- interpreting feedback as criticism

- disagreeing with co-workers

- change.

Anxiety becomes problematic if it prevents you from approaching co-workers to ask questions, or from carrying out assigned job duties, such as talking to people on the telephone, or interacting with customers. One man described his consternation at having to work in a cubicle. The thought of a co-worker entering his space unannounced so unnerved him ("What if I'm asked a question that I'm not prepared to answer?") that he became hyper-vigilant to the sound of footsteps heading his way. This was a major distraction, and the stress left him exhausted.

Andrea began a coaching session panicked about an up-coming meeting. "The vice president wants to discuss the conference that we are holding in March," she said. "I am terrified about meeting with her! I'll probably say the wrong thing and get fired."

Andrea was making negative assumptions about what *could* happen, which caused her anxiety level to rise. Knowing Andrea as I did, it was very unlikely that she would say something that would result in losing her job.

People make assumptions based on experiences from the past that they fear will be repeated in the future. They act as if their assumptions are true. Andrea's life-long difficulty answering questions spontaneously had her assuming that she would not do well in the meeting. "Usually, I know what I want to say, but I can't formulate the words," she explained. "I get flustered and blurt out whatever comes to my mind, which usually annoys people."

Andrea's anxiety was understandable. However, it was driven by an assumption. I suggested that Andrea prepare for the meeting, instead of worrying about it. I outlined a model of Information, Preparation, Practice. She agreed, and the first step was to write down *factual information*, instead of relying on assumptions, opinions or guesses.

The facts about the meeting were these:

- Four people would attend: Andrea, who handled speaker recruitment; the marketing manager; Andrea's boss, who ran the conference; and the vice president.

- Andrea had invited the vice president to make the keynote address. The purpose of the meeting was to decide the topic.

- The vice president had been with the company for less than six months, and this would be her first time at the conference.

- The marketing manager and Andrea's boss would also be participating.

Based on these facts, the next step was *preparation*. Andrea anticipated that since the vice president had only been with the company for five months, she would want to know the history of the event, this year's theme, view the agenda and learn about the attendees.

Andrea made a list of what she needed to have ready: possible topics for the keynote address; a fact sheet describing the audience, venue, and length of time the vice president would be speaking. We also prepared what to do if Andrea was asked a question that she didn't know how to answer. It occurred to Andrea that either her supervisor or the marketing manager would know what to say. "If they don't," she said, "I can tell the vice president that I'll have to research the answer and get back to her."

By this point Andrea was much calmer. Preparation increased her confidence, and helped her to feel more in control of the situation. My next suggestion was that she *practice* what she would say at the meeting. This gave Andrea the idea to review her presentation with the marketing manager prior to the meeting.

When you are feeling anxious about a situation, experiment with this problem-solving model:

- Write down the facts (not your emotions).

- Prepare a plan, based on what you anticipate will happen or be expected.

- Practice what you will say or do.

If you have difficulty with any of these steps, ask someone knowledgeable for help.

If you are in the habit, like Andrea, of anticipating negative outcomes, try challenging them with the Possible, Probable, Unlikely test:

- Write down the negative assumption.

- Ask yourself, "Is it possible that this could happen?"

- If the answer is yes, then ask, "How probable is it that this will occur?"

- If the outcome is likely to happen, ask, "How can I prepare for a better outcome?"

- If the outcome is unlikely to happen, ask, "What do I need to focus on instead?"

Here is how Andrea used this tool to challenge her assumption about the meeting:

1. Negative assumption: *I will say the wrong thing and get fired.*

2. Is it possible that this could happen? *Yes, but it would have to be something outrageous for me to lose my job.*

3. How probable is it that this will occur? *It is not probable at all. The worst I can imagine saying is that I don't know the answer to a question.*

4. How can I prepare for a better outcome? *Not applicable.*

5. What do I need to focus on instead? *Preparing the information sheet, getting some feedback from the marketing manager, and practicing what I will say.*

Depression can also be the cause of a habitually negative outlook. If you find little or no pleasure in activities you once enjoyed, have trouble sleeping, notice a change in your appetite, or feel hopeless, guilty or worthless, consult a medical professional.

MORE ANXIETY MANAGEMENT STRATEGIES

Reframing is another way to reduce anxiety. In *The Psychology of Executive Coaching, Theory and Application*, reframing is described as "an alternative context." The author notes, "The way we feel is determined by the way that we look at things, how we ascribe meanings, and what we see as the context. It all depends on how we look at it" (Peltier 2001, p.132).

If you have Asperger's Syndrome, you probably fall into the trap of black-and-white thinking. That means seeing things in one way, and not believing that there are other meanings or options. The reality is that you *can choose* to look at a situation in a more positive way. The thought that, "My projects are always late because I'm disorganized" can be reframed as, "I'm learning better time management so that my projects will be ready on time."

Reframing is *not* denying reality or making excuses. It is thinking logically about how to replace negative, self-defeating thoughts with ones that are positive *and that are also true*. A person with poor organizational skills who thinks, "From now on, I will meet every deadline," is denying reality. A person who learns how to better schedule his time and thinks, "I'm learning how to get things done on time," is reframing.

Learning to ride the wave of anxiety is another way to manage its impact. Anxious episodes come in waves. The feeling of unease builds and eventually reaches a peak, then lessens and fades away. Realizing that just when the anxiety feels the most intense, it is beginning to pass, makes it easier to cope.

Using positive self-talk can help you restore emotional calm and find solutions to problems. This is *intra*personal communication: statements that you say silently to yourself. When it is deliberate and encouraging, self-talk can lessen anxiety and help you take constructive action toward your goals.

One of Karen's big challenges was managing time. "When there's a deadline, my mind freezes," she said. "I tell myself to just forget it, the task won't get done on time." Not very encouraging thoughts! Together, we brainstormed how Karen could talk herself through situations where there were deadlines. Karen started telling herself, "You have plenty of time," and "Focus on just one thing now."

It takes time and practice to make positive self-talk automatic. My clients have reminded themselves by placing sticky notes in strategic locations, and leaving themselves voicemail messages. Karen kept her statements in a purple folder under her computer keyboard. "Every day when I see that folder, it reminds me to calm down and think instead of panic," she says.

Here are some examples of positive self-talk for various situations:

- *Preparing for job interviews*: "I am fully qualified for this position;" or "I clearly communicate my abilities;" or "I will make a favorable impression."

- *Restoring emotional calm*: "I have handled situations like this before;" or "When I'm agitated like this, I need to take a break;" or "When I am calm, I will figure out what to do." (Slow, deep breathing will also help you relax.)

- *Talking through a problem*: "Where have I seen this before?" or "The checklist reminds me of what the steps are;" or "I can revise last week's schedule, instead of starting from scratch."

- *Setting goals and monitoring progress*: "If I focus on this task for 30 minutes, it will be almost done;" or "If I rush through the cover letter, it won't get results;" or "I want to visit the gym this afternoon, so I need to finish answering emails by 11:30am."

Remember to break a project into small, manageable steps if you are becoming anxious or overwhelmed. Review the section in Chapter 5 on how to create an action plan.

Set realistic expectations. If you believe that you must do everything perfectly, your anxiety level will be high. But if you shift your focus to doing your best, assisting someone else, or learning a new skill, you will relieve yourself of a lot of pressure.

Finally, a sedentary lifestyle and large amounts of caffeine, sugar, and processed foods can overexcite the central nervous system and increase stress. A better diet and regular exercise can reduce anxiety levels significantly for some people. Anxiety can also be a side effect of some prescription medications. Consult a medical professional to review the effects of pharmaceutical drugs that you take.

Too much anxiety is counterproductive, and can be paralyzing. If you need help coping with debilitating anxiety, consult a medical professional.

SENSORY ISSUES ON THE JOB

"When entering crowded rooms or the cafeteria, the noises I hear are garbled and I can't make sense of them. It all sounds like gibberish." (Network Analyst, age 40)

"Can't you ask the cleaning people to vacuum someplace else?" Kim asked, annoyed.

Her question brought my attention to the hallway outside of my office, where I heard the faint hum of a vacuum cleaner.

"I hadn't even noticed it," I said.

Kim, incredulous, replied, "It's so loud, I can't concentrate on what you are saying."

Research has confirmed that sensory processing is a problem for individuals with Asperger's Syndrome (Myles *et al.* 2000). Difficulty with the processing or modulation of sensory information can impact many aspects of employment, and cause a great amount of stress. An individual may have problems concentrating on tasks, working in a group, understanding instructions, or taking notes. Every day, it can feel as though one is being bombarded with unpleasant sights, sounds, smells and tactile sensations. Other people might minimize or deny that there is a problem, and make insensitive remarks: "It's not that bright in here" or "Stop being so sensitive!" Most neurotypicals do not know about sensory processing problems.

There are seven sensory systems within the human body: visual; auditory; tactile; gustatory (taste); olfactory (smell); vestibular and proprioceptive (Myles *et al.* 2000). The vestibular system affects balance, and provides information about whether objects are moving, how fast, and in which direction. Proprioception allows a person to coordinate movements of various body parts, for example, to complete a task, balance, and sit in a chair without looking at it. The proprioceptive system also helps a person know how tightly to grasp objects, or how hard to push or pull an object (Myles *et al.* 2000).

One consequence of faulty sensory integration is hyper- or hypo-sensitivity to environmental stimulus. The smell of tobacco smoke on a co-worker's clothing caused Lisa to gag. Tom's co-workers were amazed when he washed out his lunch container in scalding hot water.

Coping with sensory difficulties requires forethought and planning. In some cases, problems can be mitigated with minor adjustments to a workspace, or assistive technology. Or, there may be certain occupations that are off limits. A person who is hyper-sensitive to odors should avoid working at a printing plant.

It may be necessary to formally disclose your Asperger's Syndrome and request accommodations in order to manage sensory issues. Disclosure and accommodations are discussed in Chapter 8. However, many of my clients have made their needs known without revealing that they have Asperger's Syndrome. If you chose this option, plan what you will say so that others will understand that there is a real need, and that you are not requesting special treatment. When Tara said to her supervisor, "I need a quiet cubicle so that I can concentrate," she was told, "Everyone wants a quiet cubicle!"

Use brief statements to explain the difficulty and how to solve it:

- "I have a photosensitivity and need to use a desk lamp."

- "The bright light is hurting my eyes. Can we close the blinds?"

- "My hearing is very sensitive, and the noise from the break area makes it hard for me to focus. Can I move to a different location?"

- "I am hyper-sensitive to noise. These headphones allow me to concentrate."

- "I am having a hard time following what everyone is saying. Can we write down the main ideas?"

Joseph is an attorney specializing in contract law. He tells his clients, "I need to focus on listening when you are talking, and taking notes about your situation. Please don't be offended that I am not looking at you." Meg has arranged items on her desk alphabetically so that she can find them. "I know that the scissors are always to the left of the stapler."

One way to help other people understand that you have a physiological problem is draw an analogy to something with which they are familiar. Jennifer explains her auditory processing problem like this: "I have a hearing problem that is like dyslexia. When I'm in a group, people's words get jumbled together and I can't understand them."

If you have difficulty processing group conversations, you can request written meeting notes, or a debriefing from a colleague. One of my clients arranged to attend meetings via telephone, because the amount of visual and auditory stimulation in a group was overwhelming.

There are sensory integration and assistive technologies that can improve your ability to function. Many people who have photosensitivity or other visual processing problems have found success with the Irlen Method (www.irlen.com), which uses colored overlays and filters. Noise-cancelling headphones, like those from Bose Corporation (www.bose.com), and white noise machines, are discreet ways to block or reduce background noise. The use of these technologies is becoming more and more common in "cubicle farms" (large open spaces filled with rows of cubicles).

Olfactory sensitivities can be trickier to resolve. It is unlikely that businesses will ban women from wearing perfume or men from using aftershave. However, if a particular colleague's fragrance is seriously distracting you, speak to the individual about it. Find a private space, explain the problem and make your request. You can say: "I am having an allergic reaction to your perfume. Would you mind not wearing it at the office?" Another option might be moving to a different location, away from the smell.

If you are bothered by smells in your workplace, try using a plug-in air freshener with a scent that you enjoy or can at least tolerate.

Some companies have policies restricting food consumption to the employee cafeteria or lunch room. If your co-workers eat pungent-smelling lunches at their desks, discuss this situation with your human resources representative.

ⓘ *NT Tip*
It is considered impolite to make negative comments about the smell, taste or appearance of food that others are consuming.

If your sense of smell is not very sharp, be vigilant about your own use of scented products, and your personal hygiene. Dirty clothing carries body odor. I once presented a workshop in a room that was set up for 20 participants. One of the attendees was wearing clothes that were wrinkled, stained and smelly! The odor permeated the room. Some of the other participants stood in the back to avoid sitting near this woman. If you have doubts about your hygiene, ask your work buddy whether you need to make changes and what kind.

Most people with tactile sensitivities are able to find suitable workplace attire because of the variety of fabric choices and the casual dress codes at many companies. However, shaking hands can present a problem because it is expected in so many business situations. You may be able to desensitize yourself, with practice, to tolerate a moderate amount of contact. You can feign a mild illness to avoid a handshake: "I think that I am coming down with a cold, so I won't shake your hand." This strategy will raise suspicion if it is used too often.

Another option is to use your left hand to lightly touch a person's upper right arm as you extend a greeting: "It's nice to meet you!" Keep your right arm by your side and the other person will assume that you are physically unable to shake hands.

Prepare for indoor temperatures that are too warm or too cold by layering clothing to put on or take off as needed. Small desk fans and portable space heaters may help, but check with the office manager to see if there are restrictions on their use.

If sensory processing or integration is a serious problem, consult an occupational therapist for treatment.

BULLYING AND HARASSMENT AT WORK[1]

Although bullying is often associated with being tormented in the school yard, adults can be bullied, even within the workplace. Workplace bullying (also known as mobbing or psychological harassment in some countries) is, unfortunately, a global problem.

According to a 2012 study conducted in the United States by CareerBuilder®, 35 percent of employees felt bullied at work, and 17 percent decided to quit their jobs as a result. Almost half of the workers surveyed did not confront their bullies, and most of the incidents were not reported. A global poll conducted by Monster in 2011 found the prevalence of bullying to be 65 percent of workers in the United States, 83 percent of workers in Europe, and 55 percent of workers in Asia (Cobb 2012).

Although there is no single definition, workplace bullying is generally defined as the repeated mistreatment of a worker by one or more individuals. It includes actions that are threatening, humiliating, or intimidating to the person being victimized; behaviors that prevent a person from getting his work done; and verbal abuse (Workplace Bullying Institute 2012). A bully intentionally inflicts physical or emotional harm on his victims (Attwood 2007). There is an imbalance of power, whether the bully is in a position of authority, such as a supervisor, or is an aggressive co-worker.

A bully singles out an individual, or group of individuals, for abusive treatment. This is not the same as a boss who routinely criticizes or yells at all of his staff members, or a colleague who makes hurtful comments or jokes about all or most of his co-workers. These behaviors fall into the category of

---

1   This section is for your general information, and should not be construed as legal, medical, or any other professional advice. Use your own judgment and discretion when researching information and deciding on any action related to your personal situation.

poor management and interpersonal skills, since they are not directed at a specific individual, or group of individuals.

Workplace bullying takes many different forms. Respondents in the CareerBuilder study reported being bullied in the following ways:

- Falsely accused of mistakes: 42 percent

- Ignored: 39 percent

- Used different standards/policies toward me than other workers: 36 percent

- Constantly criticized: 33 percent

- Someone didn't perform certain duties, which negatively impacted my work: 31 percent

- Yelled at by boss in front of co-workers: 28 percent

- Belittling comments were made about my work during meetings: 24 percent

- Gossiped about: 26 percent

- Someone stole credit for my work: 19 percent

- Purposely excluded from projects or meetings: 18 percent

- Picked on for personal attributes: 15 percent

(CareerBuilder 2012)

The impact of bullying can be severe, leading to health problems such as depression, anxiety, and high blood pressure. Individuals may also experience insomnia, frustration, and have difficulty concentrating on their work (Cobb 2012). In extreme cases, the result can be Post Traumatic Stress Disorder (Attwood 2007). Bullying also exacts a cost on organizations, including lowered morale and employee productivity, increased employee absences, and high staff turnover.

In many countries, bullying is not illegal. In the United States, Dr. Gary Namie, of the Workplace Bullying Institute has filed legislation with the United States Congress called the Healthy Workplace Bill (see www.healthyworkplacebill.org for more information) to create a national law against workplace bullying and intimidation. In Massachusetts, the state where

I live, State Senator Katherine Clark, in coordination with State Representative Ellen Story, has filed the Healthy Workplace Bill (House Bill 2310/Senate Bill S 916). Since 2003, 21 states have introduced this bill.

According to Senator Clark, "I have learned that workplace abuse and harassment is far too common, and that it can have both physical and psychological health consequences for employees. Further, the Commonwealth's [of Massachusetts] economic well-being depends on the success of healthy and productive employees. This bill provides two things: legal relief for employees who have been deliberately subjected to abusive work environments, and a legal incentive for employers to prevent and respond to abusive mistreatment of employees at work" (Clark 2012, personal correspondence).

At this writing in 2012, the bill has 11 co-sponsors in Massachusetts, and is endorsed by the Committee on Labor and Workforce Development. Although it did not pass during the current legislative session, Senator Clark will refile it, and expects that it will become law.

The Healthy Workplace Bill is designed to provide legal protection to individuals who are not covered by existing Federal laws that prevent harassment. According to the bill, "If mistreated employees who have been subjected to abusive treatment at work cannot establish that the behavior was motivated by race, color, sex, sexual orientation, national origin or age, they are unlikely to be protected by the law against such mistreatment."

Harassment has a different legal definition than bullying in the United States, and *is* illegal in this country. Here is the definition of harassment, from the website of the U.S. Equal Employment Opportunity Commission (EEOC, at www.eeoc.gov):

> Harassment is a form of employment discrimination that violates Title VII of the Civil Rights Act of 1964, the Age Discrimination in Employment Act of 1967, (ADEA), and the Americans with Disabilities Act of 1990, (ADA).

> Harassment is unwelcome conduct that is based on race, color, religion, sex (including pregnancy), national origin, age (40 or older), disability or genetic information. Harassment becomes unlawful where 1) enduring the offensive conduct becomes a condition of continued employment, or 2) the conduct is severe or pervasive enough to create a work environment that a reasonable person would consider intimidating, hostile, or abusive. Anti-discrimination laws also prohibit harassment against individuals in

retaliation for filing a discrimination charge, testifying, or participating in any way in an investigation, proceeding, or lawsuit under these laws; or opposing employment practices that they reasonably believe discriminate against individuals, in violation of these laws.

Petty slights, annoyances, and isolated incidents (unless extremely serious) will not rise to the level of illegality. To be unlawful, the conduct must create a work environment that would be intimidating, hostile, or offensive to reasonable people.

Offensive conduct may include, but is not limited to, offensive jokes, slurs, epithets or name calling, physical assaults or threats, intimidation, ridicule or mockery, insults or put-downs, offensive objects or pictures, and interference with work performance.

> (U.S. Equal Employment Opportunity Commission 2012a)

The law also specifically protects individuals with disabilities:

It is illegal to harass an applicant or employee because he has a disability, had a disability in the past, or is believed to have a physical or mental impairment that is not transitory (lasting or expected to last six months or less) and minor (even if he does not have such an impairment).

Harassment can include, for example, offensive remarks about a person's disability. Although the law doesn't prohibit simple teasing, offhand comments, or isolated incidents that aren't very serious, harassment is illegal when it is so frequent or severe that it creates a hostile or offensive work environment or when it results in an adverse employment decision (such as the victim being fired or demoted).

The harasser can be the victim's supervisor, a supervisor in another area, a co-worker, or someone who is not an employee of the employer, such as a client or customer.

> (U.S. Equal Employment Opportunity Commission 2012b)

In Europe, bullying often falls under general laws that compel employers to provide safe working environments for their employees (Cobb 2012). Some countries, such as Denmark, France, the Netherlands, Norway, Serbia, and Sweden, have enacted specific laws against bullying (Cobb 2012).

In most jurisdictions in Canada, laws against violence in the workplace also cover bullying, although Quebec has specific legislation covering "psychological harassment" (Canadian Centre for Occupational Health and Safety 2005).

WHAT TO DO IF YOU ARE BULLIED OR HARASSED

Bullying can happen to anyone. People engage in bullying behavior for a variety of reasons. Usually, a bully is insecure, and victimizes others in order to appear strong and in charge. Jealousy of a co-worker can motivate a bully to undermine the victim's accomplishments so that his status is elevated in the eyes of colleagues (Fast 2004). The individual may have been bullied himself, and believe that this is acceptable behavior.

Individuals with Asperger's Syndrome can be easy targets for bullies. The fact that you are different, or seen as vulnerable, can make you a target. A difficulty with social communication, and interpreting the motives and actions of others, can provide the bully with a convenient excuse: "She's too sensitive" or "He has it all wrong!" A lack of relationships with co-workers who can come to your defense also makes you more susceptible. The confusion and anxiety about communication in general, and conflict in particular, make it less likely that Aspergians will report incidents.

There are several actions you can take if you believe that you are being bullied or harassed at work.

First, be sure that you are not misinterpreting innocent jokes or attempts by co-workers to be friendly. Maura became extremely angry and felt humiliated when a colleague made a pun based on her last name. The remark was made at a holiday party, by a co-worker she had gotten along well with for three years. Viewed within that context, Maura later agreed that her co-worker had simply been joking, and had no intentions to upset her.

Do not confuse performance feedback with bullying or harassment. James believed that his civil rights were being violated after his supervisor asked him to talk less at meetings, and avoid bringing up subjects that had already been discussed. There is nothing untoward or illegal about setting rules and agendas for meetings.

If a colleague says or does something that you don't like, you could decide to attribute the incident to a misunderstanding, and let it go. People sometimes make insensitive remarks, without realizing or intending to be unkind. If you have a tendency to be very literal, or hyper-sensitive to any perceived criticism, you might be overreacting. Put the situation into a broader context, and consider where and when the incident happened, and your relationship with the person(s) involved. Remember that isolated incidents, offhanded remarks and teasing do not meet the legal definition of harassment.

It can be helpful to get advice from someone you trust, such as your work buddy, or someone outside of the office such as a therapist or coach.

If the incidents occur several times, or are serious, you should speak with the individual involved. Do this in a private place, such as a conference room or a private office. Do not begin the conversation with accusations or angry remarks. If you say, "Your rude, nasty comment that I 'don't get it' was completely out of line. Knock it off!" the other person will become defensive. If you have misunderstood the person's intentions, such accusations will make you seem unreasonable.

Instead, be calm, and avoid judgments or blame. One of my favorite models for confronting people about their behavior is from the book *Find Your Focus Zone*. The steps are:

1. State the facts.

2. Say how you feel.

3. See the situation through the other person's eyes.

4. Ask for what you want.

(Palladino 2007, p.116)

Here is an example of how this model works: *"When you say that I 'don't get it'* [the facts], *I am concerned that others will think that I'm not qualified for my job* [how you feel]. *I realize that I tend to take things literally* [seeing the situation through the other person's eyes, in this case assuming that there was no ill intention], *but I'd like you stop making that remark"* [what you want].

You may need assistance in applying this model, particularly when it comes to imagining the other person's perspective. If you decide to confront a co-worker, do so within 48 hours of the original incident. Otherwise it may appear that you are holding a grudge.

If confronting an individual is impossible for you, or unpleasant incidents continue, or someone says or does something outrageous, it is time to involve human resources and/or your supervisor. Many companies have formal policies and procedures concerning bullying and harassment. These will be described in the employee handbook.

If the problem is with your supervisor, you obviously will need to speak with someone in human resources. This is a good idea even when the problem is with a co-worker. Human resources professionals are trained in how to address such complaints. They can guide you on how to document incidents, will investigate your complaint, and can mediate between you and the other person(s) involved. Sometimes, the human resources manager will arrange sensitivity training for employees. Professionals like myself, and autism organizations, often provide training to companies about Asperger's Syndrome.

It is possible that reporting bullying or harassment will make the situation worse. Anger or fear of job loss can make a perpetrator even more aggressive, in subtle ways that are hard to prove. He may have allies within the company who will defend his actions, or discredit information from the victim. Other employees, fearing retribution, might not report incidents that they have witnessed. The environment can become very unpleasant and stressful, and often, work performance suffers.

In situations like these, you might ask to transfer to another department or division within the company. Or, you might decide to look for another job. For some people, the stress becomes so debilitating, that they quit without having another job. Try to avoid this unless it is absolutely necessary, as it will make it harder for you to get hired elsewhere.

If you believe that you have been unlawfully harassed, legal action is an option. Lawsuits are stressful, time consuming, and very expensive. They can take years, and there is never a guarantee that you will win. If you want to explore this option, seek an attorney who specializes in employment and/or disability law. In the United States, you can file a complaint with the Equal Employment Opportunity Commission (EEOC), or an appropriate state agency. For more information, visit www.eeoc.gov. Readers in other countries should consult the local or government agency that is responsible for workplace health and safety.

Finally, be aware that neurotypicals can feel bullied and harassed by the actions of Aspergians. Blunt remarks, harsh criticism, and angry outbursts can make others feel demeaned and intimidated. Remarks about a person's race, religion, or country of origin, or actions that can be interpreted as sexual harassment, can be grounds for a disciplinary action or dismissal.

CHAPTER 7

MANAGING YOUR CAREER

After earning a Master's degree from one of the finest schools in the country, Evan began his career in engineering.

Things did not go smoothly at his first job. He was shocked when his work was rejected outright, since he believed that he had followed his supervisor's instructions to the letter. Working in a small office, surrounded by other people, for 50 to 60 hours a week was also proving to be a strain. He began to intentionally alienate his colleagues by making negative comments about their hobbies and interests. He was fired within six months.

His next position seemed ideal because he was able to work in nearly total isolation. Once, he didn't have to speak to anyone else in the company for two weeks. Then he began reporting to a new supervisor. He was instructed to "give customers a religious experience," which was a completely meaningless directive to Evan. He was fired after three months.

At the next job, he was again flummoxed by responsibilities that included becoming a "product evangelist" and "leveraging the brand." Discouraged, he withdrew his energy from the job, and was fired yet again.

When his fourth position ended the same way, Evan realized that he needed to make changes. His employment goal was to earn a steady income and stay with a company long enough to earn a promotion. He asked a former co-worker to help him figure out what was going wrong.

"I realized that my job was to execute ideas from the creative team," Evan said, "and that if I wanted to stay employed, I had to figure out what they wanted." When he landed his next job, he clarified instructions. He also improved his communication skills. "It took extraordinary effort, but I started talking to people during the day and made positive comments in meetings." He also learned about working as part of a team. "If I received something late, I didn't assume that everyone would know that *my* work would be late as a result." If colleagues didn't comment on a proposal, Evan no longer assumed that it meant that they agreed with it. He began following up and asking for feedback.

After more than four years with this company, during which he earned a promotion and received two salary increases, Evan accepted a more challenging opportunity with another firm. "This is the first time that the choice to move to another company was mine," he says.

There are two parts to managing your career. The first is meeting expectations and interacting effectively with your colleagues so that you maintain steady employment. Multiple job losses not only impact your earning power, but often lead to a loss of self-esteem and depression.

The second part of career management is professional development. This includes keeping your skills up to date, or improving them. Paying attention to industry trends helps you recognize opportunities and make better career decisions. Awareness of your strengths, as well as your limitations, enables you to choose jobs that emphasize what you do well.

BUILD ON YOUR STRENGTHS

"It's easy to be negative and think about all the things you find difficult. Try and be positive instead and remind yourself of all the things you can do and the things that you can learn to do. You are not disabled, you just have differing abilities." (Manufacturer's Representative, age 39)

Building on your areas of strength is important career advice for everyone. For individuals with Asperger's Syndrome, it is imperative that you find work that emphasizes your areas of ability. Let's face it, you probably will not be able to compete for jobs based on salesmanship, political savvy, or leadership. However, you can compete on the strengths of the Asperger mind. These are generally recognized as:

- the ability to sustain focus and concentrate on tasks for extended periods of time

- strong long-term memory, particularly for facts and details

- deep knowledge of specialized topics

- accuracy and attention to detail, particularly noticing errors or inconsistencies

- objective, logical analysis of situations

- creativity and innovative thinking

- persistence, especially when completing tasks

- honesty and loyalty.

I think of neurotypicals and Aspergians as satisfying two distinct needs with the workplace. Neurotypicals are the multitasking generalists, with broad skill sets, who focus on the big picture. Aspergians are the experts and technicians, with an eye for detail.

Specialisterne is an innovative software testing company that was founded in Denmark by a man whose son has Asperger's Syndrome. Specialisterne is Danish for "the specialists." Its business model is based on utilizing the cognitive strengths of people with Asperger's Syndrome and high-functioning autism. The company specifically hires people on the autism spectrum because their focus, attention to detail, and precision make them better software testers than most neurotypicals. Specialisterne's clients include Microsoft and Oracle. Founder Thorkil Sonne has established the Specialist People Foundation with the goal of creating one million jobs for "Specialist People" around the world. (To learn more, visit www.specialisterne.com.)

Specialisterne is expanding, and in 2012 entered the United States. The Specialisterne model, and other organizations that are adapting it, will be discussed in more detail in Chapter 9.

Michael Burry is a physician-turned-hedge-fund-manager who has Asperger's Syndrome. His research into the subprime mortgage market enabled him to predict the subprime crisis two years before anyone else saw it coming. Scion Capital, Burry's firm, shorted the market, and earned several hundred million dollars for its investors. Burry was profiled in *The Big Short: Inside the Doomsday Machine*. Author Michael Lewis writes, "He didn't talk to anyone about what became his new obsession: he just sat alone in his office…and read books and articles and financial filings" (Lewis 2010, p.136). You can learn more about Michael Burry at michaelburryblog.blogspot.com.

You may not be interested in software testing, or reach the prominence of Michael Burry. However, you can look for ways to capitalize on your strengths so that they outweigh your limitations in the eyes of an employer.

I have worked with clients in their 40s and 50s who have no idea where their talents lie. Often they are in careers that emphasize their challenges instead of their assets. Even when this is apparent to the individual, some are so uncomfortable with change that they stay in jobs that drain their energy, and leave them in constant fear of being fired.

Several of my clients have earned the respect of their co-workers due to their superior technical ability. One young man convinced an employer to overlook a requirement for one year of work experience, by demonstrating his in-depth knowledge of a particular type of machinery.

Create a profile of your strengths by writing down the following:

- *Talents*: things that you are naturally good at, such as writing, drawing, teaching, researching, analyzing, or designing.

- *Skills*: competencies that are learned and developed over time, for example, accounting, computer programming, oil painting, medical coding, or welding.

- *Personal characteristics*: qualities such as honesty, persistence, intelligence, patience, creativity, and loyalty.

- *Education*: degrees, certificates, and apprenticeships, as well as attendance at workshops and conferences, and knowledge which is self-taught.

Once you understand what your strengths and abilities are, you can formulate a plan for building upon them. Denise works as an occupational therapist at a private clinic. She is very good at teaching. She developed a workshop that was so popular among patients that the director of the clinic decided to offer it to the public. It brought new clients to the clinic, and resulted in an expanded role for Denise, creating educational programs.

Cate noticed that her manager spent a lot of time training employees on a complicated data entry process. She volunteered to write an instructional manual, an activity that utilized her writing skills.

Marc volunteered his programming skills to build a website for his church. One of the congregation worked for a technology company, and offered Marc a job based on his volunteer work for the church.

Developing your talents and skills is something that you do over the course of your career. Here are some ideas of how:

- Update your skills through workshops, classes or certificate programs.

- Join a professional association. You can volunteer on a committee, contribute articles to newsletters or a website, write guest blogs, or speak at an event.

- Attend industry conferences.

- Read professional publications to stay current on industry trends.

- Participate in online groups that are related to your occupation.

One caveat: when building on your strengths, be sure that you do not neglect other critical employment skills. You probably will not work in isolation, like Michael Burry. Every improvement you make in interpersonal communication, organization, and time management will pay off many times over.

ACCEPT YOUR LIMITATIONS

Every human being has limitations. Some of my clients are concerned that admitting weaknesses means that they are "less than" others or that they cannot be successful. Others do not want to acknowledge that they are not suited to certain jobs, and continue to have bad employment experiences.

I believe that the more you understand about Asperger's Syndrome and how it impacts *you*, the easier it will be to sustain employment. It is my experience that the work environment can be as, or even more, important than job tasks. *Preferences* for neurotypicals, such as a quiet workspace, low-pressure atmosphere, and clear performance expectations may be *necessities* if you have Asperger's Syndrome.

I see two categories of limitations. There are limitations that can be mitigated by learning new skills, utilizing assistive technology, or receiving workplace accommodations (disclosure and accommodations are discussed in the next chapter). The second category is limitations that you can't do much to change. These can steer you away from occupations that would be difficult or impossible to manage.

Some individuals with Asperger's Syndrome have a slow brain processing speed. It takes them longer to interpret information from their senses, and decide how to act on it. Slow processing speed is a category two limitation, since processing speed cannot be changed. For these individuals, a job that requires taking in information from several sources simultaneously, analyzing it, and making a quick decision would be very difficult. Similarly, a person who has poor working memory will not do well at a job that requires rapid attention-shifting.

The Checklist of Common Workplace Challenges will help you identify challenges that may interfere with your performance. There may be areas that you need to address on your own. If you frequently offend co-workers with inappropriate remarks, to the degree that it impacts productivity, you may need to invest in coaching or communication skills training. Or, you may need accommodations from your employer. If you misinterpret instructions because you are very literal, it might be reasonable to request step-by-step instructions for certain tasks.

✓

CHECKLIST OF COMMON WORKPLACE CHALLENGES

1. Communication Challenges:

   ☐ Take instructions literally and miss implied meanings

   ☐ Unintentionally offend others with blunt/inappropriate statements

   ☐ Unable to maintain adequate eye contact

   ☐ Speak too rapidly, loudly or softly

   ☐ Talk too much

   ☐ Interrupt others often

   ☐ Difficulty initiating or sustaining conversations with co-workers

   ☐ Don't notice, or misinterpret, nonverbal signals, causing misunderstandings

   ☐ Unaware of own facial expressions and body language (forget to smile; look angry when you are not)

   ☐ Afraid or unsure of how to ask for help

   ☐ Other communication challenges: _____

   _____

   _____

2. Executive Function Challenges:

   ☐ Unsure of how to begin tasks or projects

   ☐ Underestimate how long a task will or should take

   ☐ Become lost in details, losing sight of the purpose of a task

   ☐ Don't see options (continue to do what isn't working)

   ☐ Easily distracted

✓

- ☐ Forget what needs to be done, or the sequence of steps in a process
- ☐ Forget verbal instructions
- ☐ Work too slowly
- ☐ Unsure of how to prioritize projects
- ☐ Difficulty multitasking (rapid attention-shifting)
- ☐ Unsure of expectations, or what a finished product should look like
- ☐ Appear not to take initiative because next steps are not clear
- ☐ Ask too many questions
- ☐ Act impulsively, based on too little information
- ☐ Resist change or the ideas of others
- ☐ Insist on doing things a certain way
- ☐ Other executive function challenges: _____

_____

_____

3. Sensory and Motor Challenges:

- ☐ Visual sensitivity: _____
- ☐ Auditory sensitivity: _____
- ☐ Olfactory sensitivity: _____
- ☐ Tactile sensitivity: _____
- ☐ Auditory processing problems
- ☐ Fine motor problems (difficulty writing, stuffing envelopes)
- ☐ Gross motor problems (difficulty coordinating movements)
- ☐ Other sensory/motor challenges: _____

_____

_____

4. Emotional Challenges:

☐ Difficulty controlling anger or frustration

☐ Cry too often, or over minor difficulties

☐ Highly anxious

☐ React defensively to criticism

☐ Other emotional challenges: _____

_____

_____

HOW TO TELL IF YOU ARE IN THE WRONG JOB OR CAREER

Brendan felt trapped in his job as a project manager. Over the previous 16 months, his role had changed to involve much more interaction with co-workers in other departments. While his knowledge of company processes was vast, Brendan's understanding of company politics was limited. He was unsure of how to influence colleagues so that his projects were priorities. When deadlines were missed, or mistakes were made, Brendan sent angry emails.

Brendan's company had a "people first" culture where collaboration and teamwork were highly valued. After receiving several complaints about Brendan's abrasive style, his supervisor initiated a disciplinary action. "Now, I have to be hyper-vigilant about not saying the wrong thing," he explained.

It became increasingly difficult for Brendan to manage the workload, people interaction, and stress. He came home from work completely exhausted, but had trouble sleeping through the night. After one particularly trying day, I revisited a subject that we had discussed before.

"Is this the right job?" I asked. "It seems that now, one of your primary responsibilities is developing and maintaining relationships with people in many different departments. Even though they don't report to you, you are responsible for seeing that they complete certain tasks on time. Interpersonal communication is the area that is most difficult for you."

"No!" Brendan exclaimed in an angry tone, "This isn't the right job. But I can't leave. I'm too tired when I get home to look for another job. I don't interview well, so no one will hire me, anyway. The job I really want requires a doctorate, and there is no way I can work and pursue a degree at the same time. I've *tried* changing careers, and nothing works. The only option I have is to find a way to survive this job."

Once, after being laid off, Brendan had attempted to change careers. A single meeting with a recruiter convinced him that he needed a doctorate. This one attempt to find a more manageable career happened 16 years ago. It was still hard for Brendan to conceive of what he could do differently today.

I notice this kind of rigid mindset often, especially when individuals are stressed. They see no options, and no hope for a better outcome. Jack refused to visit the website of a very large, international corporation because he insisted that they were not hiring.

"When was the last time you checked?" I asked him.

"Three years ago," Jack said.

Peter chose accounting after taking a career assessment. With much difficulty, he earned a Master's degree in accounting, and managed to pass the CPA exam.

In six years, Peter had been fired from four jobs. At each one, he made too many errors, and did not prepare tax returns quickly enough. "I am so worried about making a mistake, that I check and recheck my work," he said. His organizational skills were also a problem. Peter frequently misplaced files, failed to follow through with client requests, and forgot staff meetings.

Peter had a hard time fitting in with his colleagues, and believed that they didn't like him. A few had complained that he asked too many routine questions. Peter admitted that his real passion was teaching, not accounting.

When he began coaching, Peter said that his goal was to find yet another accounting job. When I questioned that choice, he admitted that he disliked change, and often stayed with things even when they were not working.

Individuals can find themselves in the wrong career, like Peter. Or, they can be at the wrong job, like Brendan. Signs that you are in the wrong job or career include:

- being fired three times or more, from the same type of job, for the same reasons

- consistently having difficulty managing your workload; assignments are often incorrect or late

- working much longer hours than your colleagues

- spending most of your time on tasks that are difficult, instead of those you do well

- being drained and exhausted at the end of each day

- becoming involved in a serious conflict with a supervisor or co-worker that cannot be repaired.

Do not allow stress to make you rigid in your thinking, or paralyze you. If you do not see options, or reject every suggestion as unworkable, you are being rigid. Usually, this is due to fear.

Many skills are transferable to different jobs or industries. Anna left the high-pressure environment of technology start-ups to produce corporate communications for a manufacturing firm. Peter decided to explore options for teaching accounting. Brendan began checking his company's intranet to see whether he could transfer to a job that required less interaction with others.

You do not necessarily have to earn another four-year degree, or an advanced degree, to change careers. It is quite possible that you can qualify for a different line of work through a certificate or vocational training program that can be completed in a few months.

To explore career options, I recommend the Occupational Outlook Handbook (www.bls.gov/ooh). This is a database produced by U.S. Department of Labor that you can access at no charge. It describes all types of occupations, including the primary tasks and responsibilities, work environment, educational requirements, and employment outlook. You can search your current job, then click on the link to related careers. You might find occupations that are similar to what you do now, but more suited to your abilities. If you live outside the U.S., search online for "occupational information" to find resources for basic career research in your country.

I often recommend two books from JIST Publishing: *200 Best Jobs for Introverts* (Shatkin *et al.* 2008), and *300 Best Jobs Without a Four-Year Degree* (Farr and Shatkin 2009).

Although it is not a career tool, an up-to-date neuropsychological evaluation offers valuable information for career planning. Widely used in the diagnosis of Asperger's Syndrome, it measures cognitive abilities in areas such as attention, memory, language, visual-spatial abilities, and executive functioning. The results can be helpful in choosing occupations that maximize strengths, and minimize areas of weakness. These evaluations are usually performed by a clinical neuropsychologist, who includes vocational recommendations.

SHOULD YOU BE A MANAGER?

After four years of updating medical records, Wes was ready for a new challenge. When his supervisor asked whether he was interested in being a manager, he answered with an enthusiastic, "Yes!" In addition to more responsibility, he would receive a larger paycheck.

Within his first month, Wes was overwhelmed. He had to oversee the work of three specialists. Although they did not report to him, Wes had to be sure that they met productivity requirements. When errors were made, managers in other departments contacted Wes, not the specialists. He often felt irritated by what seemed like their careless mistakes.

Wes was also put in charge of updating the records management system. He found the many meetings he attended to be confusing, and had difficulty understanding the requirements of users in various departments. He knew that the new system couldn't meet everyone's ideal, but wasn't sure what functionality was critical. Several times, when Wes asked his supervisor a question, he was told, "We already discussed that."

The stress of interacting with so many people, and the pressure to manage multiple tasks, began to wear on Wes. He wished to have his old job back.

When Bob started coaching, his goal was to show his boss why he should be promoted from senior manager to director.

"Let's start with the reasons that you want this promotion," I suggested.

"Well, I graduated from an Ivy League school, so I should be a director," Bob said. "People will respect me, and I'll make more money. I've been with this company for six years, and two of my colleagues were promoted to that level."

I pointed out that Bob had not mentioned anything about the actual job responsibilities. He admitted concerns about navigating corporate politics, and his ability to work at a strategic level.

"There are some people that I won't be able to get along with," Bob said. "They are bullies and liars, and I refuse to work with people like that."

Frank, on the other hand, was in charge of a small group of engineers. He had the role for more than three years. Although the job was stressful, he enjoyed it, and received positive performance reviews.

The employees that Frank managed were, like him, talented, experienced and self-directed. "We speak the same language," he explained. "My boss knows that I am not good with 'people stuff.' She handles the sales and marketing groups, and I concentrate on developing the products."

Almost all of Frank's interaction was with fellow engineers. When he did meet with individuals in sales and marketing, his supervisor was there to translate their requests and concerns. Frank was a manager who was able to focus on his area of strength: engineering.

Not everyone is cut out for a management role. During my corporate career, I saw many sales people who were promoted to sales manager. Many did not succeed. Their skill was selling products and services. Once they were managers, they did very little selling, and much more forecasting, budgeting, and reporting. Most became frustrated because they were doing what they disliked the most: paperwork; and not doing what they liked best: interacting with customers and selling.

People can have the job title of manager, and oversee processes. The primary focus is on handling facts and information, not interacting with others. In most cases, however, a title of manager, director or vice president carries with it a requirement for sophisticated levels of interpersonal communication.

Here are some things to consider about being a manager:

- *The higher your rank in an organization, the more important people skills become.* There can be interaction with employees in different departments, senior management, as well as with outside vendors or service providers. Various individuals will have different perspectives, objectives, motives and needs. It will be necessary at times to interact professionally with people you don't like, and to deal with office politics.

- *Management is about the big picture, not the details.* Rather than executing tasks, the emphasis is on overseeing the work of others, planning strategies, handling administrative duties, such as reporting and budgeting, and ensuring that operations run smoothly.

- *Decision-making is part of managing.* Managers must sometimes make unpopular decisions, for the overall good of the company. Decision-making involves evaluating relevant data from many sources, weighing options, considering the impact on others, and taking responsibility for outcomes.

- *Managing direct reports is a tough job.* It includes motivating people to do their best work, resolving conflicts, managing workloads, providing feedback, and conducting performance reviews. If employees think that their work isn't valued, or that their supervisor is not supportive, they will look for different jobs. High staff turnover reflects poorly on a department manager.

Before you accept a job as manager or director or vice president, think carefully about your ability and desire to interact with other people, handle administrative functions, and oversee rather than execute.

PERFORMING A SWOT ANALYSIS

A SWOT analysis is a tool that can help you evaluate your abilities, your current career direction, or other employment options.

SWOT is an acronym that stands for **S**trengths, **W**eaknesses, **O**pportunities, and **T**hreats. It is used frequently in business for strategic planning. You can perform your own personal SWOT analysis.

In addition to your own assessment, you can ask people who know you for their evaluation. These can be family members, a friend, mentor, coach or other professional. Comparing your responses to those of others can provide a clearer picture of your situation, and options.

The four SWOT questions are:

1. *What are your strengths?* These include personal attributes plus resources that give you an advantage. List the following:

   a) Things that you do well, such as talents and specific skills.

   b) Personal characteristics such as honesty, persistence, and intelligence.

   c) Education, which can include formal degrees or vocational training, as well as certificates, continuing education workshops, internships, and knowledge that was self-taught.

   d) People you know who can help you reach your career goals. This can include current and former co-workers, college professors or alumni, fellow members of a professional association, vendors or service providers you do business with, and family members.

   e) Other resources, such as having the time and money to return to school, or access to specialized equipment.

2. *What are your weaknesses?* This encompasses personal limitations as well as external factors that can impact on your employment. List the following:

   a) Personal difficulties, such as organizing time, remembering appointments, multitasking, managing anger, anxiety, etc.

   b) Job-related skills that you need to acquire or improve. These can be hard skills, such as learning computer applications, as well as soft skills like being punctual, interviewing, interacting with co-workers, or asking for help.

c) External factors such as multiple job losses, no references, a large gap in employment, work experience that doesn't match education (e.g. Master's degree, but employed as retail sales associate), limited mobility (e.g. no access to public transportation).

d) Unrealistic expectations about opportunities, your qualifications or your salary requirements.

3. *What are your opportunities?* These are the positive potentials available to you. Describe:

a) Industry trends or regulatory changes you can capitalize on; opportunities for advancement at your current company; networking contacts who can help you transfer to a different industry.

b) Opportunities for state- or employer-sponsored training.

c) A new company or industry being started or moving to your area.

4. *What threats do you face?* List the obstacles that are getting in the way of your employment goals, such as:

a) Weaknesses or unrealistic expectations from question 2 that you must address.

b) External factors, such as a new technology, that are making jobs obsolete; new job responsibilities that do not match your abilities.

A SWOT analysis enables you to identify opportunities that you haven't considered, and areas that you need to address to maximize your chances for success. On the next page is a SWOT analysis template.

✓

SWOT ANALYSIS

SWOT stands for **S**trengths, **W**eaknesses, **O**pportunities, and **T**hreats. Complete the four questions below. You can also ask people who know you well for their evaluation.

1. *What are your strengths?* These include personal attributes plus resources that give you an advantage.

   a) Talents and skills: _____

   _____

   _____

   _____

   b) Personal characteristics: _____

   _____

   _____

   _____

   c) Education (degrees, certificates, workshops, internships, self-taught): _____

   _____

   _____

   _____

   d) People who can assist you: _____

   _____

   _____

   _____

e) Other resources: _____

_____

_____

_____

2. *What are your weaknesses?* This encompasses personal limitations as well as external factors that can slow or derail your employment search.

a) Personal difficulties: _____

_____

_____

_____

b) Missing or inadequate skills or knowledge: _____

_____

_____

_____

c) External factors: _____

_____

_____

_____

d) Unrealistic expectations: _____

_____

_____

_____

3. *What are your opportunities?* These are the positive potentials available to you.

   a) Industry trends or regulatory changes to capitalize on: ____

   _____

   _____

   _____

   b) Growth industries in need of my skills: _____

   _____

   _____

   _____

4. *What threats do you face?* List the obstacles that are getting in the way of your employment goals.

   a) Weaknesses or unrealistic expectations from question 2 that must be addressed: _____

   _____

   _____

   _____

   b) External factors: _____

   _____

   _____

   _____

WHY YOU NEED TO NETWORK, EVEN WHEN YOU'RE EMPLOYED

Nearly every one of my clients actively avoids networking. Often, it is associated with walking into a room full of strangers and striking up a conversation. You may be surprised to know that there are many ways to network that do not involve crowds, strangers, or being unsure of what to say.

People equate networking with a job search, however, it is also a valuable activity when you are employed. Networking contacts can help you advance your career, and offer advice and resources to help you perform your job better.

The value of networking is its efficiency. You are connecting with other people to share information, much like a computer network allows many users to share files. Every person you connect with knows other people, who in turn know people, and on and on. This chain of connections makes it much easier to get information. When I needed a meeting space for eight weeks, I contacted four professionals in my network. In less than 24 hours, I was put in touch with the owner of a private practice. One email later, I had a space. *That's* efficient!

Networking is a reciprocal exchange. People are willing to contribute their time and resources in anticipation that you will return the favor, if or when asked. It capitalizes on the fact that people like to do business with people they know, and generally like to help others. There is also a tacit endorsement when someone makes a referral. If I recommend a service provider to a client, *my* reputation is on the line. Therefore, I only make referrals to professionals I know.

This is a tale of two clients. Both work in the high-tech industry. Both were laid off unexpectedly. Joe went home and immediately began searching the job boards and sending out resumes. Lots and lots of resumes. Steven went home and sent out emails to 20 of his business contacts. Within 48 hours, one told him about an opening at a company that had tried to recruit Steven previously. Steven contacted the hiring manager,[1] and two weeks after being laid off, accepted a job offer.

Meantime, it was week four of Joe's search. He met with a recruiter, and realized that he could not supply three references, as requested. Emails that he sent to former co-workers bounced back. When he did manage to locate them at their new companies, his queries went unanswered. It had been three years

---

1   Hiring manager refers to the person who makes the decision about who to hire, not a human resources manager. The hiring manager is nearly always the individual you will report to.

since he had spoken with one, and four and a half years since he had spoken with the other. "They may not even remember me," he thought. The lack of references was slowing down his job search. Joe was concerned that he would not be able to locate three people who would speak positively about his work.

Networking is not only for job seekers. It is an activity that will be useful throughout your career.

Diane was a graphic artist who was eager to find a field that paid better than the publishing industry. She wondered whether she could transfer her skills to the marketing department of an information technology company. "I'm unsure about how much I need to understand about computer technology," she said. "I wish I knew someone in the industry." Diane realized that speaking with someone who was working in the technology field would help her discover whether she could transfer her skills.

Phil had recently been assigned to program an innovative piece of software. It was a high-visibility project that could put him in line for a promotion. His supervisor commented multiple times about the slow pace of Phil's work. Although Phil assured him that he was on schedule, the project was falling behind. Phil wasn't familiar with the new programming tools, nor were his co-workers. His calls to the manufacturer's technical support staff weren't solving the problems. "I wish I could get advice from a programmer who has actually used these tools on a project like mine," he thought. "It would save so much time, and I would get the answers I need." Phil was missing out on tips and suggestions from fellow programming professionals that could save him time, and help him work more efficiently.

An excellent place to start networking is with the people you already know. These can be current and former co-workers; vendors that you do business with; college alumni and professors; acquaintances from your religious organization, volunteer activities, or a hobby group; and family members.

Stay in touch with former co-workers you got along well with previously. This can be as simple as sending a friendly email to inquire about how they are, or suggest meeting for lunch or coffee. Your outreach does not have to be frequent. An invitation every few months or once a year is usually enough (unless, of course, you both enjoy getting together more often). It is important that you express a genuine interest in learning about how the person is doing. If you contact people only when you need a favor, they will not want to stay in touch with you.

You can also utilize an online business networking site, such as LinkedIn (www.linkedin.com). Create a profile and invite individuals you know to join your network. This way, you can send status updates on a periodic basis. People may invite you to join their networks as well. You can access the basic LinkedIn service at no charge.

The updates you post should be business related. Avoid discussing your personal relationships: "I'm getting a divorce." Also refrain from negative comments about other people or your company: "My boss is a complete jerk" or "This company doesn't care about its employees." This not only makes you look unprofessional, it will turn off employers who regularly search LinkedIn profiles seeking job candidates. You never know who is going to read what you have written.

Appropriate topics for updates include: announcing a promotion or a new job; additional training that you have received; a link to an interesting business article; the industry conference that you are attending; or a business-related book or blog that you recommend.

Read the updates that your connections share, and respond with a note when appropriate: "Congratulations on your promotion;" or "Good luck in your new job;" or "Thanks for passing on the excellent article."

LinkedIn hosts thousands of online industry groups. These allow you to participate in discussions with other professionals, ask questions and make new contacts. There is no charge to join (or start) a group.

The LinkedIn Learning Center provides more information about how to use this networking tool.

While some people have business relationships that span decades, it is more likely that you will lose touch with some individuals over three or four years. The important thing is that they are replaced by new people who you have met and added to your network. You should always be looking for new professional contacts.

PROFESSIONAL ASSOCIATIONS

A professional association is an organization of individuals who work in the same industry, or at the same type of job. There are associations of informational technology professionals, journalists, marketing professionals, paralegals—you name it. These organizations promote professionalism, keep members updated on industry and career news, and may sponsor conferences, workshops or training. Typically, there is a monthly meeting that includes time for networking, and a presentation on a topic that is relevant to members.

Associations are good places to expand your professional network. The events are structured, and all of the people attending have something in common. Although there is a social component, people expect to discuss business topics. You may enjoy the chance to discuss aspects of your work with others in your field. Some of my clients volunteer on committees, so that they can meet members while performing a particular job, such as distributing name badges.

Prospective members can usually attend one association meeting at no or low cost, to evaluate whether they would like to join the group. Often, existing members are encouraged to bring colleagues to a meeting. Perhaps one of your networking contacts can escort you to a meeting and make some introductions.

In the United States you can expect to pay from one to several hundred dollars a year for membership. The fee might be deductible from your income taxes. Check with your accountant, if you have one, or with the tax office. Or, your employer might reimburse you.

Prepare in advance for an association event. Visit the group's website to familiarize yourself with its mission, history and activities. This will help you prepare questions to ask when you meet people during the networking session: "How long have you been a member of this association?" or "Are you familiar with tonight's speaker?" or "What kind of work do you do?"

If you are very anxious about talking to people you don't know, plan to arrive just in time for the formal presentation. After you are seated, challenge yourself to speak to the person on your right and the person on your left, even if you ask just a single question. You must practice in order to become comfortable and confident talking to new people.

MORE WAYS TO NETWORK

If you write well, submit articles for publication to trade magazines or industry websites or blogs. Insightful, well-written material can build your recognition and credibility in your field and can lead to job offers.

Speaking at industry events is another way to make connections. Check association websites and trade magazines for information about up-coming conferences. These programs are often planned nine months to a year in advance. Ask to be placed on the list for submitting proposals to speak.

Having an interest in your work makes it easier to attend industry events and make contact with colleagues. Some people who have little interest in socializing discover that they enjoy interacting with other professionals to discuss industry news and share ideas. If you are currently working in an area that is not satisfying, find ways to interact with people who share a personal interest of yours. This is also a way to network. Ryan found a data entry job through a friend he met who shared his interest in Anime (Japanese animation).

Networking requires consistent effort over time, so choose activities that you will continue. Attending a single association meeting, or writing one blog post every few months, will not yield results. Do at least one activity that involves face-to-face meetings; this is how the most meaningful connections are made.

ANATOMY OF A 30-SECOND ELEVATOR SPEECH

An "elevator speech" (also known as "elevator pitch" or "commercial") is a brief summary of who you are and what you do. It is used as a means of introduction at various business events. It is so named because it is brief—you can say it in about the time it would take to ride an elevator from the bottom to the top floor of a building. In practice, an elevator speech is usually 30 to 60 seconds.

Job seekers use elevator pitches to describe their qualifications and explain what kind of work they want. Individuals who are employed use their "commercial" at networking events, professional conferences and in other business situations.

An elevator pitch from an individual who is seeking referrals or business contacts might sound like this:

> "My name is Mike Smith and I work for Corporate Photography Studios. We specialize in photography for annual reports, corporate brochures and websites. My clients include ACME Company and LM Widgets. Recently I was at the Town Machinery Company photographing 12 members of the management team and their new factory. Do you know of any marketing directors I should get in touch with?"

When introducing yourself to an individual during the networking portion of a business event, you should use a less formal, more conversational style: "Hello, my name is Bob Johnson. I'm a programmer at ABC Software." The other person will introduce himself, and probably ask you a question. It is expected that you answer the question, and ask about or comment on the same or a related topic.

These networking exchanges often last for three to five turns. Like this:

Bob: "Hello, my name is Bob Johnson. I'm a programmer at ABC Software. We specialize in applications for media development."

Mary: "Hi, Bob. I'm Mary Wright, and I head the marketing group at DataComputation Associates. We consult to Fortune 1000 companies. Is this your first time at a Tech Professionals Association meeting?"

Bob: "Yes. I am eager to meet some other people in the field. A colleague at work spoke highly of this group. Have you been a member long?"

Mary: "For three years, and I have met a lot of very interesting and talented people here. What kind of projects do you work on?"

Bob: "Right now I am writing code for some new multimedia software. You don't happen to know of someone who has worked with the MegaBuilder program, do you?"

Experiment with different versions of your "pitch" until you are comfortable saying it. Avoid too much descriptive language, as it makes you sound phony: "I am a technology-savvy, results-oriented marketing manager…" Practice saying your pitch out loud, so that you sound confident.

WHAT TO DO IF YOU ARE FIRED

"University doesn't prepare you for real life work culture." (Administrative Assistant, age 31)

Involuntary job loss is a stressful experience that erodes self-confidence and self-esteem. Getting fired ranks eighth out of 43 stressors on the Holmes and Rahe Stress Scale, which measures the impact of various events on an individual's sense of well-being (Holmes and Rahe 1967).

Job loss is hard on everyone. It can be particularly hard if you have Asperger's Syndrome. You may not understand why you were terminated, which makes it difficult to know what to do differently in the future. Difficulties with interpersonal communication may have led to misunderstandings that your employer interpreted as willful behavior. The job may have emphasized your areas of challenge, instead of your strengths. You may lack basic job readiness skills that must be mastered before you are employable.

Whether you have been fired once or multiple times, job loss does not diminish your value as a person. It has to do with your skills and abilities not being the right match for a particular position. What is important is to learn as much as you can about what went wrong, and what changes you need to make.

Even if you didn't enjoy your work, getting fired is a personal loss, and it is normal to feel sadness, anger, confusion, and fear. Find someone to talk to so that you do not become overwhelmed with emotions. Depending on the circumstances of your termination, you may be eligible to collect unemployment insurance. If you live in the United States, check with your state unemployment office.

There are some lucky individuals who receive specific feedback about why they were let go. I say "lucky" because they now know what areas they need to develop. This information is much more useful than vague reasons, such as not being a team player, or being hard to get along with.

It is sometimes possible to contact a former supervisor or a former colleague to clarify why you were let go. Do this to find out what you need to correct, not to argue for why you should get your job back. Initiate the contact within one week of being terminated, via telephone or email. *Do not* visit your former place of employment without prior approval. If your request is denied, accept it and do not ask again. If your job ended after much conflict, it is best not to contact anyone in the company, unless it is to discuss an administrative issue concerning health insurance benefits, unemployment claims, or a final paycheck. Contact the human resources department about administrative items.

These are common reasons for job loss, and suggestions about skills that you may need to develop. Consult the appropriate chapters in this book for suggestions regarding specific skills and situations.

- *Employer said that you were rude, difficult to work with, not a team player.* Improving your communication skills should be a priority. If they cost you one job, they very likely will cost you another. Do you need to learn how to make small talk, so that you can establish good working relationships with others? Or, do you need to change the way that you give feedback to colleagues? "Difficult to work with" and poor teamwork can mean: continually challenging the ideas of other people; not listening to instructions; not following procedures; being defensive about feedback or criticism.

- *You thought that everything was fine, and were completely shocked to be fired.* You probably missed signs that there were performance problems. Neurotypicals will not explain things that are considered obvious. They assume that you understand things as they do. In the future, clarify assignments and check in with your supervisor at regular intervals about your performance. If something isn't clear, ask, don't guess. You are being told that you are not meeting expectations with phrases like: "You shouldn't have to ask that;" or "we went through this already;" or "you didn't listen." Ask your peers for ideas about how to be more efficient on the job.

- *You lost your temper, said or did something inappropriate, had a serious conflict with your supervisor or a co-worker.* It is my experience that these are chronic problems that usually result in multiple job losses. You must learn to manage your anger, frustration and stress. Think seriously about your career choice: are you in a field that is too demanding or that requires too much interaction with others? Perhaps you have unrealistic expectations about your decision-making or other authority. Do you feel contempt for people who you believe are not as intelligent as you are?

   It bears repeating that functioning well within a group is a basic workplace requirement.

- *You were bored or unhappy with your work and stopped trying, became chronically late, or refused to follow instructions.* Termination is never desirable because it creates a situation that must be explained during job interviews. If you are unable to continue in a job, resign and give your employer a minimum of two weeks' notice before you leave. No matter what your personal feelings are about the company or the people in it, do your best to leave on good terms. That means acknowledging that things did not work out and leaving without incident. You never know when you might work with someone again, or need a reference.

- *The quality of your work was fine, but you were unable to meet productivity requirements.* Identify where the problem lies. Perhaps you spent too much time on non-essential tasks, or beginning projects from scratch instead of using templates or established procedures. Maybe you tried to make every project "perfect," which took time away from other duties. If you do not understand the purpose of a task, it can be difficult to learn and remember what to do. Do you need written, instead of verbal, instructions? At your next job, find a work buddy who can help you prioritize and find shortcuts.

  If low productivity has resulted in the loss of two or more jobs, you may be in the wrong kind of work, or at the wrong type of company. Food service jobs, for example, require multitasking, good working memory and speed. Some customer service positions require dual-track processing—listening to a customer while simultaneously typing notes into a computer database. Some industries are known for high pressure and tight deadlines, for example, high-tech start-ups that are financed by venture capitalists.

  You may need to retrain. Find a career coach or counselor, preferably one who understands Asperger's Syndrome, to help you to figure out what jobs are a good match. Identify jobs in fields that are growing and in need of skilled workers.

- *You were confused about expectations, asked too many or too few questions, and did not take initiative.* Learn how to clarify performance expectations, and how assignments should be done. Ask what you should do once assigned tasks are completed. Being idle is associated with laziness and low motivation. If your anxiety is severe enough that you don't ask questions, or avoid certain tasks, seek professional help.

WHAT *NOT* TO DO IF YOU ARE FIRED

Matt called me in an emotional roil. After weeks of conflict with his supervisor, he had been fired. In frustration and anger, he had yelled in the hallways about how unfair his boss and the company had been to him. He threatened to contact a lawyer to discuss suing the firm. Matt was escorted from the building by security personnel. He wanted my opinion about his plan to picket the company for depriving him of a livelihood.

We discussed how picketing the company would alienate his former colleagues, whom he would need as references. It might also lead to his arrest. Negative publicity would cause other companies to avoid hiring him.

To my relief, Matt ended the call by thanking me for helping him see that picketing the company would be a huge mistake that could negatively affect his career for years to come.

Matt's situation illustrates why it is never a good idea to act when you are agitated or angry. People literally do not think clearly when they are highly emotionally aroused (see Chapter 6 for an explanation of the amygdala hijack).

Difficult as it may be, accept the news of termination quietly. Do not yell, curse, cry, call people names, beg for your job back, or accuse the company of discrimination. If you threaten injury to a person, or company property, you could be arrested.

Vent your emotions privately, away from the workplace. Do not take any action until you are calm. People who are expecting to be terminated may be unperturbed by the news. It can even be a relief.

If the reason for your job loss is poor performance, or company cutbacks, you may be eligible for unemployment benefits. You will not be eligible if you were fired for misconduct, such as lying or stealing. In the United States, guidelines vary by state. Contact your state unemployment office, or appropriate government agency, for information.

If you believe that you have been discriminated against, in the United States you can contact the Equal Employment Opportunity Commission (www.eeoc.gov) or an attorney who specializes in employment law.

Do not take any action until you have had a chance to discuss the situation with someone you know and trust.

HOW TO RESIGN

People voluntarily leave their jobs for many reasons. Most often, it is because they have found a job with another company. They could leave for personal reasons, such as wanting to spend more time with children, or because they are returning to school.

Sometimes, high stress, great difficulty meeting performance expectations, boredom, or conflicts with colleagues prompts a person to resign. Individuals who believe that they are about to be fired may resign so that their exit is voluntary.

If your employment experience has been unpleasant, it is tempting to vent anger and frustration, particularly if you are leaving for another job. While this might be cathartic in the short term, it is not a good idea for your career. Unless it is truly unavoidable, you should leave an employer on good terms.

Don't burn your bridges is an excellent piece of business advice. It means to avoid saying or doing anything that will irrevocably damage your reputation or relationship with the company. Telling your boss that he is incompetent; ranting to management about how much you hate the company; or simply walking out are examples of burning bridges.

You never know when, or under what circumstances, you will encounter these co-workers again. People change jobs and careers. Companies are bought and merged. A peer at your current company may become a hiring manager at another. If you are perceived as unstable or irrational, your colleagues will not maintain contact. They certainly will not provide references for you.

It is customary to resign to your supervisor. If there has been a conflict, then do so with the human resources manager. Ideally, submit your resignation in person. Otherwise, provide a typewritten letter. It is my opinion that email is too informal. If you do tender your resignation in person, you should also provide a signed, written letter.

Two weeks' notice is standard in the United States, unless you have an employment contract that says otherwise. Individuals in senior management positions are expected to give notice of at least one month, or until the company can find a replacement. Follow the guidelines that are customary in your country. Count your notice by the business week, which is Monday through Friday. If your employer asks you to leave earlier than you had planned, do so. Commonly, people resign on either a Friday or a Monday.

Keep your comments brief. If you decide to state the reason that you are leaving, do so in neutral or positive terms: "I've accepted an offer with another firm;" or "I've decided to pursue an M.B.A. full time;" or "I am exploring other opportunities that will be a better match for my skills." Express gratitude for the experience, unless there has been a conflict, in which case you can express disappointment that things didn't work out.

Here is an example of a polite, basic resignation letter:

February 22, 2013

Ms. Jill Lawson
Marketing Director
ACME Widgets, Inc.
555 Main Street
Anytown, USA 54321

Dear Ms. Lawson:

This is to inform you that I am resigning from my position as data entry clerk effective March 8. I have decided to accept an offer with another firm that will further my career goals.

I enjoyed working for ACME Widgets, and learned a lot during my two years with the company. I regret any inconvenience this may cause, and will do my best to have all of my current assignments finished before I leave.

If I can be of any help during this transition, please let me know.

Sincerely,

Alex Smith
22 Maple Street
Anytown, USA 12345

CHAPTER 8

DISCLOSURE AND ACCOMMODATIONS

"Accommodations have made a huge difference in how I cope and perform at work." (Network Analyst, age 40)

Clients often ask my opinion about whether they should disclose their Asperger's Syndrome to an employer. My reply is, "It depends." Disclosure is a personal decision. Whether it is the right option for you depends on the nature of your job, your overall performance, specific challenges that you face, whether you have had a disciplinary action, and your comfort level with disclosing a disability.

If you live in a country that has anti-discrimination laws, such as the Americans with Disabilities Act (ADA), disclosing to an employer offers you certain protections. Some of my clients who were in danger of losing their jobs received accommodations that enabled them to meet performance expectations. The risk is that a job offer could be rescinded, a promotion denied or a job lost, without the real reason being stated. It can be difficult, expensive and time consuming to prove discrimination.

What follows is a brief overview of the Americans with Disabilities Act as it pertains to employment. Readers outside of the U.S. should consult their local laws regarding discrimination.

The ADA states that employers must provide equal opportunities to *qualified* individuals in hiring, firing, promotions, compensation, training and development, benefits, and other employment practices. A qualified individual is someone who meets the employer's requirements for education, skills, experience, and work performance.

This is an important point to understand. Employers do not have to lower their standards of quality or productivity for an employee who is disabled. Let's suppose that all customer service representatives are expected to enter a minimum of 30 orders per hour. Because of Asperger's Syndrome, your processing speed is slower; you can only enter 22 orders. You would be considered unqualified for the job.

Disclosing does not guarantee that you will receive a job offer or continue in your current employment. The law does not compel an employer to hire someone *because* he has a disability. It says that disabled individuals cannot be denied opportunities to obtain and maintain employment.

An employer is compelled to make reasonable accommodations for qualified individuals with disabilities. An accommodation is a modification or adjustment that allows a person to participate in the interviewing process, or to perform the essential functions of their job. The modification must be realistic and cannot cause an undue hardship for the employer.

The definition of what is reasonable depends on your job and the company. For Susan, a data entry clerk, requesting written instructions was reasonable. Ken, however, worked as a financial analyst. His supervisor explained that Ken's job required judgment. It was not possible to provide written instructions about how to address every possible situation.

An undue hardship at a company with 25 employees might not be considered an undue hardship at one with 10,000 employees. Modifications that would incur significant cost or disrupt an aspect of the business would be considered an undue hardship for the employer.

Here are examples of workplace accommodations that my clients have asked for and been granted:

- use of laptop for note-taking during meetings

- meeting notes taken by a colleague

- weekly meetings with supervisor to clarify expectations and identify priorities

- written instructions for tasks and procedures

- lobby television turned off during shift

- non-essential scheduling tasks reassigned to co-worker

- permission to take breaks when overly stressed

- requests from staff members submitted in writing

- interview questions submitted in advance

- switch to a technical job, from a management role

- move to a quiet workspace

- use of headphones to block out noise.

A further protection for employers is that an employee with a disability must be able to perform the essential functions of their job, or they can be fired. Essential job functions are the core tasks and responsibilities for which you are hired. For an accountant, using standard accounting software would be considered an essential function. If you have visual-spatial problems that make it impossible for you to use spreadsheets, you would be considered unqualified for the position. However, if you are a copywriter, entering budget information into spreadsheets once or twice a year may not be an essential function of your job. You can request, as an accommodation, that tasks involving spreadsheets be reassigned to someone else.

There is a difference between accommodation and basic job readiness. A person with a disability can request a modification in work hours, if, for example, he must use public transportation to travel to work. However, an employer does not have to excuse someone who arrives late to work because he has difficulty managing his time.

Employers do not have to accommodate employees who pose a direct threat to the health or safety of themselves or others, or those who engage in serious misconduct. Losing your temper at work can be considered a direct threat. Jack's work situation deteriorated over several months. He would frequently storm out of department meetings, muttering under his breath about procedures he didn't like. He exploded at one meeting, yelling at his co-workers about his Asperger's Syndrome and why it made it hard for him to interact with others. When his boss denied Jack's request to use vacation time, Jack sent him a threatening email. Jack was promptly fired.

Employers are prohibited from asking questions about a medical condition or a disability on employment applications and during job interviews. After an offer of employment is made, an employer *can* ask medical and disability-related questions as long as they do this to everyone who is offered the same kind of job. Once you start work, an employer cannot ask disability-related questions, unless they are related to your job or are necessary in order for the employer to conduct business. Suppose your supervisor notices that you seem dizzy when you stand up. Your job requires you to operate machinery. In this case, the employer has a reasonable belief that you have a disability or medical condition that could pose a risk to your safety, and that of others, and can ask questions about your health.

You are under no legal obligation to disclose. If you choose to do so, your employer can request proof of your diagnosis from a qualified medical professional. They can also inquire about how, specifically, your disability impacts your job performance. Many companies have a form for your medical provider to fill out. You can, and should, control what information is given to an employer. It is not necessary, or desirable, to submit your full neuropsychological evaluation, or your entire medical history. Ask your medical professional to restrict comments to those items that affect your ability to perform your *current* job.

It is beyond the scope of this book to fully describe the Americans with Disabilities Act and the criteria for being considered disabled. Readers in the United States are encouraged to visit the website of the Job Accommodation Network (JAN; www.askjan.org) for a detailed discussion of anti-discrimination laws. JAN is a service of the U.S. Department of Labor's Office of Disability Employment Policy, and provides free information and consultations. Readers in other countries should consult the appropriate government agency. If you believe that you have experienced job discrimination, consult an employment law attorney.

The ADA does not contain a list of specific accommodations. Instead, accommodations are decided on an individual basis. Most employers are very willing to make adjustments that are reasonable.

DISCLOSING IN A SOLUTION-FOCUSED WAY

The ADA applies to all phases of employment, from submitting a resume or application, to interviewing, and job tasks and opportunities after you are hired.

If you disclose, it is important that you do so in a solution-focused way. Your manager and human resources representative may know little or nothing about Asperger's Syndrome. Making a general statement, such as "I have Asperger's and can't multitask," puts the burden of figuring out an accommodation on the people who know the least about what you need.

Proactively suggesting solutions greatly increases the likelihood that your employer will implement them.

Requesting accommodations is a *negotiation*. An employer does not have to comply with your request, if it would cause an undue hardship, or interfere with the productivity of yourself or others. A company is within its rights to offer an alternative accommodation that will address your need.

Do not approach this as a battle. Making demands, and threatening legal action if they are not met, puts the employer on the defensive, and usually results in a poor outcome. Be professional, and demonstrate a positive attitude and willingness to compromise. Do not act in an unreasonable manner.

I have developed a three-step process for planning a disclosure strategy:

- Step 1: Determine *what* to disclose.

- Step 2: Decide *how* to disclose.

- Step 3: Choose *when* to disclose.

- *Step 1: Determine what to disclose.* Write down each challenge that you face, its impact on your performance, and the accommodations that you believe will solve the problem. Focus only on those challenges that impact you during the hiring process or at your current job. Do not list difficulties related to your personal life or schooling. You may want to refer to the Checklist of Common Workplace Challenges in Chapter 7.

  Here are examples:

Challenge: Slower information processing makes it difficult to answer interview questions in real time.

Impact: Unable to organize thoughts, and communicate abilities to the employer.

Accommodation/s: Receive questions in advance of an interview.

*

Challenge: Learning new, multistep processes quickly.

Impact: Overwhelmed by too much information; forget verbal instructions.

Accommodation/s: Break training into smaller segments; receive written instructions.

*

Challenge: Prioritizing tasks and projects.

Impact: Too much time is spent on non-essential tasks; important deadlines are missed.

Accommodation/s: Daily review of priorities with supervisor.

- *Step 2: Decide how to disclose*. Your disclosure statement should be short, simple and to the point. Do not launch into a long explanation of the history of Asperger's Syndrome, theories about its cause, or all of the potential difficulties. Avoid jargon or terms that will be confusing and raise questions about your ability to do the job.

  Trevor received a job offer and was concerned that his difficulties with social interaction might impact his performance. He drafted a two-page letter to the hiring manager that included quotations from the *Diagnostic and Statistical Manual of Mental Disorders*, which is used by clinicians to make diagnoses. Not only did his letter contain many details that were irrelevant to the workplace, it is highly unlikely that his future supervisor would understand terms like "restricted repetitive and stereotyped patterns of behavior" (American Psychiatric Association 2000, p.84). The letter also described "weird things" that Trevor did, including stimming, which he was able to control in public. Since he could control his hand flapping, there was no reason to discuss it. "Weird" is a poor word choice, because weird behavior makes people nervous.

  When Lesley disclosed she explained, "I have Asperger's Syndrome, a neurological condition that makes it hard for me to remember verbal instructions. During training, I need to make notes, and practice the steps in order."

- *Step 3: Choose when to disclose*. There are pros and cons to disclosing at different stages of the employment cycle. The best time to disclose depends on your situation. Here are benefits and risks to consider.

Disclosing in Your Cover Letter or When Submitting a Job Application

Generally, I do not advise disclosing at this stage, because doing so puts the focus on potential problems, rather than your qualifications. In many organizations, there is still apprehension about hiring people with disabilities. One concern is that the individual will require an inordinate amount of training or supervision. Another is that accommodations will cost a lot of money, even though according to a JAN study, more than half of accommodations cost nothing, and the rest cost $500 or less (Job Accommodation Network 2005).

A third concern is that the company will be sued for discrimination, if an employee cannot meet performance requirements and is terminated.

However, if you need assistance submitting an application, or with the interview process, you must let the employer know beforehand. Ann had significant difficulty making eye contact, remembering to smile, and making any type of small talk. Trying to appear neurotypical on interviews caused her so much stress that she couldn't focus on answering the questions.

Ann disclosed her Asperger's Syndrome in the cover letter that she submitted with her resume. She had been referred to the hiring manager by the friend of a family member. With Ann's permission, the friend mentioned to the hiring manager that Ann has Asperger's Syndrome. Ann's cover letter mentioned her disability briefly, and put it in a positive light. It read in part, "Please be assured that my disability will not interfere with my ability to do this job, and in some ways, will actually be an asset. I am very reliable, and am driven to do an extremely good job. I urge you to speak with my former supervisor…"

During the interview, Ann addressed her difficulties with making eye contact and remembering to smile by saying, "I don't show a lot of emotion because of the Asperger's Syndrome. However, I am very enthusiastic about this position and brought a summary of successful projects to discuss." The summary was a bulleted list of achievements in her past positions. It helped her remember points about her qualifications that she wanted to make during the interview. She was hired on a three-month trial basis.

Another reason to disclose Asperger's Syndrome at the application stage is when it offers a distinct advantage. If you are applying for a position with an autism association, for example, your personal understanding of Asperger's could be helpful in the development of programs or educational materials. Even so, Asperger's should not be the main focus of your cover letter and resume—your skills and experience should be.

Disclosing During a Job Interview

Generally, I do not advise disclosing at this stage, either. The purpose of an interview is to demonstrate your capabilities and explain how you can contribute to the company's success. Disclosure can get in the way of this by focusing attention on your limitations and on potential problems.

However, if your challenges are so noticeable that not offering an explanation will disqualify you from consideration, disclosure is a viable strategy. Slow processing speed meant that Allison needed several seconds to organize her thoughts before responding to questions. This could make Allison appear "spacy" and unprepared. She decided to tell potential employers, "Because of my Asperger's Syndrome, I need a few seconds to organize my thoughts in order to answer your questions."

Disclosing When You Receive a Job Offer

The purpose of disclosing is to request an accommodation. If you believe that you can meet the employer's performance expectations, there is no reason to disclose Asperger's Syndrome. You can always disclose after you are on the job, if you realize that you need a modification in order to be successful.

It is advisable to disclose if you know that you will need a significant accommodation immediately. In the United States, an employer cannot rescind a job offer because you disclose a disability. An employer could understandably feel deceived if you wait until your first day to ask for a modification. It begins your working relationship in an atmosphere of distrust. Finding the right moment to disclose would also be awkward. The employer would be prepared to get you started on the job, not to modify your workspace or reassign non-essential tasks.

Dan's technical skills were outstanding, but he had a history of job loss, and wanted to try a new approach after his latest termination. He identified his problem areas and accommodation needs. Then, after receiving a verbal job offer, but before signing an employment agreement, Dan told his would-be manager that he has Asperger's Syndrome. He described how Asperger's affects his ability to understand body language and how he can sometimes appear rude to people. He mentioned that he would need help with prioritizing and estimating how long a project should take to complete. It turned out that his supervisor had a family member on the autism spectrum. Dan was able to focus on learning the job, instead of worrying about what to do first and by when.

Disclosing After You Have Started Work

This is the stage where most of the individuals I coach make a disclosure. Usually, the precipitating event is negative feedback from a supervisor, conflict with a co-worker, receiving a disciplinary action, being put on a Performance Improvement Plan (PIP), or having two weeks' notice to improve, which almost always means that you are going to be fired.

It might also be in your interest to disclose if:

- your work is consistently late or has to be redone

- you receive feedback about the same performance problem three times or more

- you are confused about expectations

- you cannot perform an aspect of the job.

On the following page is a rating scale that can help you determine whether to disclose.

The wrong time to disclose is in a moment of panic because you made a mistake or had an argument. Cathy nearly talked herself out of a job when she blurted out to a human resources manager that Asperger's Syndrome made it hard to remember faces, multitask and deal with interruptions: all basic skills for a receptionist!

✓

DISCLOSURE NEED AND ACTION SCALE

Readers have permission to download this template for personal use, from www.jkp.com/catalogue/book/9781849059435/resources.

How Serious is the Problem?	*Possible Action Steps*
Level 3: Immediate Action Required ☐ Formal disciplinary action; probation or two weeks' notice to improve ☐ Formal meeting with supervisor about performance problems; written warning; placed on Performance Improvement Plan	☐ Disclosure and formal accommodation request ☐ Engage a professional to intervene on my behalf ☐ Other: _____ _____ _____ _____
Level 2: Corrective Action Needed ☐ Same performance problem has been mentioned more than twice ☐ I am consistently redoing assignments ☐ Assignments are late on a regular basis	☐ Disclosure and formal accommodation request ☐ Talk to supervisor about difficulties; suggest solutions without formal disclosure ☐ Ask a co-worker for ideas about improving performance ☐ Evaluate whether this is the right job or career ☐ Other: _____ _____ _____

✓

Level 1: Needs My Attention	☐ Ask a co-worker for ideas on improving performance
☐ Working very long hours	☐ Meet regularly with supervisor to clarify priorities and expectations
☐ Confused about what is expected	
☐ Continually rechecking work; forgetting steps	☐ Use checklists; make notes
☐ Told that I am asking too many questions/should know what to do by now	☐ Request additional training
	☐ Find ways to manage stress and anxiety
☐ Anxious and unsure about performance	☐ Other: _____
	_____
	_____

DOS AND DON'TS OF DISCLOSING

It is possible that problems can be addressed without disclosing a disability. Developing a repertoire of explanatory statements may be enough to "neutralize" unexpected behaviors and smooth over misunderstandings. You could explain: "I'm hyper-sensitive to office noise and wear headphones so that I can concentrate;" or "I need to write the steps down in order to remember them;" or "I tend to be literal; let me know if I am missing the point."

Asking to see a sample of what a completed project should look like, or to review priorities each week with your supervisor, will not be seen as unusual requests in most cases.

If your requests are treated as preferences, and not taken seriously, formal disclosure may be necessary. Even if you have been treated badly, or blamed for a misunderstanding, approach disclosure in a professional manner. Dramatic proclamations that you have been abused, tortured or persecuted can make you appear mentally unstable and immature. It is imperative that you speak to your supervisor and human resources representative when you are calm.

Be certain that what you need is an accommodation, and not a different type of job. Sean wanted me to speak with his employer about accommodations. He worked in a warehouse and had received a written warning about his performance. He frequently forgot one or two steps in the process of sorting and moving shipments. He was also not keeping pace with the other workers. As we discussed the situation in more detail, Sean said that the noise and activity in the warehouse were very distracting. He described himself as "thorough and slow moving."

I asked Sean what accommodations he needed. He wanted to wear headphones during his shift, and to work at a slower pace. The headphones were a problem because Sean needed to hear when a forklift was behind him. Instructions were often called out to workers by the supervisor. Slowing his pace wasn't an option since everyone needed to work at the same speed to move materials efficiently.

It was apparent that the warehouse position was simply not a good match for Sean. He was unable to meet the requirement for speed, or to consistently follow verbal directions. He agreed that he needed to find work that matched his abilities.

A disability is not an excuse for disruptive behavior. Tyler was placed on a Performance Improvement Plan (PIP) for losing his temper and cursing at a co-worker. "I can't help it if Asperger's Syndrome makes me explosive," he said. Although I agreed that low frustration tolerance is common among people with Asperger's Syndrome, Tyler still needed to control his temper in the office. One condition of his PIP was that he receive coaching to learn how to lower his stress level and manage frustration. (See Chapter 6 for information on managing anger, frustration, anxiety and stress.)

You must be willing to follow through when you agree to change an unacceptable behavior. By the time Tyler was placed on the PIP, there had been two other inappropriate outbursts. Tyler's employer made it clear that he needed to change his actions, or he would lose his job.

It can be helpful to offer your supervisor and human resources representative a brief article about Asperger's Syndrome. Do not expect them to read a book about the subject. There is an Asperger's Syndrome Guide for Employers in the appendix of this book. Readers may download and photocopy the guide for the purpose of educating their employers.

When you disclose, mention the things that are going *well* on the job, and state your commitment to excellent performance. Be sure to emphasize your expertise and abilities. There are a number of strengths associated with Asperger's Syndrome that are benefits in the right job. They include:

- Attention to detail and sustained concentration.

    Benefits: ability to spot errors; accuracy; not distracted from the task at hand.

- Excellent long-term memory.

    Benefits: recall facts and details others have forgotten.

- Tolerance of repetition and routine.

    Benefits: perform the same tasks without getting bored or burned out.

- Strong logic and analytic skills.

    Benefits: ability to see patterns/connections in data; objective view of facts.

- Vast knowledge of specialized fields.

    Benefits: develop in-depth knowledge and expertise.

- Creative thinking.

    Benefits: different way of processing information can lead to novel solutions.

- Perseverance.

  Benefits: stick with a job until it is done.

- Honesty and loyalty.

  Benefits: not afraid to tell the truth; stay with an employer long term.

It is preferable to have a discussion when you disclose. If you are absolutely unable to explain your situation verbally, you can do so with a written letter. It is prudent to follow up verbal disclosure with a written document. It should summarize what was discussed in your meeting and what everyone agreed will happen next.

Disclosing to your supervisor and human resources representative does not give them permission to tell other people in the company about your diagnosis. You control who has access to this information. If you want it kept confidential, state this clearly. If there are other people in the company whom you want to know about your Asperger's Syndrome, state specifically who those individuals are. Check that disclosure information is kept in a separate file from your general personnel records. That way, if you leave your current employer for any reason, the information will not follow you to another company.

EXAMPLES OF DISCLOSURE STRATEGIES

The following examples illustrate different disclosure strategies. They underscore the importance of a "custom-crafted" approach that addresses the needs of the individual as well as the demands of the job.

For nearly ten years, Cindy was a successful sales manager at a luxury vacation community. Despite her Asperger's Syndrome, she did well working one on one with clients and training junior sales people. Her group often ranked number one or number two in quarterly sales.

After the company was acquired by a much larger firm, Cindy's job became less structured. She received conflicting instructions from various executives in the organization. The new regional vice president said that Cindy asked too many questions, and gave too much detail in her presentations. At weekly team meetings, Cindy appeared chronically unprepared to answer questions from the executives.

Concerned about her performance, Cindy decided to disclose her Asperger's Syndrome to her supervisor and human resources representative.

Her accommodation requests included receiving a written agenda one day in advance of the team meetings. She also asked that managers submit their questions to her in writing, and give her 24 hours to respond. These accommodations addressed auditory processing problems that made it hard for her to follow group discussions. They also mitigated her slow processing speed, which made it impossible for her to respond immediately to questions from managers. After implementing the changes, she was able to participate in the meetings and provide the responses the management team needed.

Cindy also requested an extra week to learn new processes. Her supervisor began giving her written directions, specific examples, and more of his time to answer her detailed questions. Instead of giving Cindy a vague instruction like, "Take the numbers and run with it," her supervisor began stating specifically, "Write a ten-minute presentation, based on this quarter's sales reports, that will explain where we can increase revenue."

Cathy is a receptionist for a large financial firm. One of her duties is to make sure that visitors have the proper security clearance before exiting the lobby area and entering the building. One particularly busy day, Cathy issued a visitor badge to someone she thought she recognized as he rushed through the checkpoint and quickly flashed an ID. Concerned about the possible security breach, Cathy reported the incident to her supervisor, who issued Cathy a written warning.

Cathy explained to human resources that Asperger's Syndrome affects her short-term memory, and her ability to recognize faces under stress. Her employer agreed to turn off the television in the lobby during Cathy's shift, because the sound is distracting to her. Employees were instructed to send written, not verbal, visitor requests to Cathy in advance, so that she will have more time to process them. Signs are now posted in the lobby informing visitors that they must check in with the receptionist and show appropriate identification.

Todd contacted me as he was having an employment crisis. Employed in a director-level job for two years, his literal interpretation of instructions and difficulty seeing the big picture were frustrating his colleagues. Todd's supervisor expected him to assume "a leadership role," a directive that was completely bewildering to Todd. When we met, Todd had been given two weeks to improve his performance or be fired.

Todd disclosed his Asperger's Syndrome and, over the next three months, Todd, his manager and a human resources representative decided accommodations and set clear performance expectations. Then an opportunity arose for Todd, at his own request, to give up his director position and become a senior manager instead. He realized that as a manager, he would utilize his considerable technical ability, and not have to worry about leadership and people management duties. By acknowledging his strengths and limitations, Todd's status changed from about-to-be-fired to valuable member of the company.

A final example is Adam, an extremely bright program manager at a major, international conglomerate. He was consistently praised for his extensive knowledge of supply chain management, and his organization's systems and processes. Like many people with Asperger's Syndrome, Adam is a perfectionist and can be impatient with those who don't share his knowledge and very high performance standards. Easily frustrated, he regularly engages in heated debates about minute points.

Adam was upset to learn that his acerbic communication style and detail focus had raised doubts about his ability to work with others and to think strategically. He was denied a promotion to director, and started coaching to learn how to give feedback without alienating his colleagues. He continued to struggle with inter-department politics and strategic thinking. At issue was whether he can meet the demands of a director-level job. He elected not to disclose his Asperger's Syndrome to his employer, and is uncertain about whether to pursue a promotion.

Sometimes, despite disclosure and your best effort, you lose your job. If this happens, or has happened, to you, treat it as a learning experience. Try to find out specifically what went wrong, and what you need to improve. Research other industries or professions where you can transfer your skills. Do not become discouraged. With determination and practice, virtually everyone can learn new skills and gain insight into their strengths and limitations. This increases the odds of finding satisfying employment. (See also the section on "What to Do if You are Fired" in Chapter 7.)

CHAPTER 9

IN THE FINAL ANALYSIS

I notice that a lot of attention is being focused on the topic of employment for individuals on the autism spectrum. In some ways, it seems that neurotypicals have suddenly realized that children grow up, and they don't outgrow autism. For autistic individuals who are able to work, employment can mean independence, and provide a sense of purpose and belonging.

The number of autistic individuals has grown so large that neurotypicals are being forced to take action. It is estimated that 200,000 teenagers on the autism spectrum will become adults by 2016, in the United States alone (Harmon 2011). Not all of them will be able to work. Those who can, along with the individuals who have already reached adulthood, represent a large pool of capable people who can answer the need among employers for skilled, loyal workers.

Specialisterne, the company that I mentioned in Chapter 7, pioneered the concept of creating jobs that capitalize on the strengths of autistic individuals. Specialisterne is Danish for "the specialists." It was founded in Denmark in 2004 by Thorkil Sonne, whose son has Asperger's Syndrome. Sonne realized that in addition to challenges, his son has specific strengths. Sonne recognized that software testing is an occupation that utilizes many of the cognitive strengths of individuals with Asperger's Syndrome and high-functioning autism.

Specialisterne specifically hires people on the autism spectrum because their focus, attention to detail, and precision make them better software testers than most neurotypicals. The company's clients include Microsoft and Oracle. Specialisterne is expanding operations throughout Europe, and in 2012 entered the United States. Thorkil Sonne established the Specialist People Foundation with the goal of creating one million jobs around the world for "specialist people" with autism and similar challenges. (To learn more, visit www.specialisterne.com.)

Other organizations are following suit. Aspiritech (www.aspiritech.org) is a non-profit company in Illinois that has adapted the Specialisterne model. According to their literature, Aspiritech employs testers who have "…unique and exceptional software testing abilities, including: A fundamental enjoyment for software testing—thriving on tedious tasks; excellent attention to detail; incredible precision and extensive focus; [high intelligence and] strong technical skills."

Semperical, based in California, has developed a "cloud-based" Virtual Workplace Platform that will enable individuals around the world to log onto the internet, and work as contractors from home. Initially, Semperical will focus on software testing jobs, but plans to expand the model to other occupations. At the time of this writing, Semperical plans to begin hiring in the spring of 2013.

Of course, not everyone with Asperger's Syndrome is interested in the high-technology field, or in working for one of these organizations. However, the positive publicity they generate promotes understanding of what individuals with Asperger's Syndrome are capable of in the workplace.

This may not be a great comfort if you are struggling to find a job, or are having difficulty meeting the expectations of your current employer. However, until the day that "Aspergian-friendly" companies are the norm, rather than the exception, the burden is on you to fit in.

I encourage you to adopt Thorkil Sonne's "dandelion philosophy." He says that, depending on your point of view, a dandelion is either a valuable herb or an invasive weed. "A weed is a beautiful plant in an unwanted place," Sonne says. "An herb is the same plant where it is wanted" (Bornstein 2011).

See yourself as an herb: talented, capable, and with much to offer the world. The most successful clients I know are the ones who accept themselves, and their Asperger's Syndrome. They use their experiences, both positive and negative, to learn about themselves. They do not give their power away by blaming other people for their difficulties, or constantly focusing on what is wrong. Instead, they push themselves to learn new skills and grow. And, they do not give up.

Things *can* change. My client John has experienced much hardship in his life, including a devastating personal loss. He initially contacted me in desperation because he was about to be fired. John disclosed to his employer, and received accommodations that enabled him to perform his job successfully.

In a stroke of good fortune, he began working for a new manager, who appreciated his expertise.

John also changed the way that he interacted with his co-workers. Rather than fighting against the expectations for teamwork and collaboration, he forced himself to listen more, and stopped making negative remarks.

Now, several years later, John is a well-respected professional in his field. He has an excellent job, and finds personal fulfillment in his special interest. He started exercising and lost weight, eats better, and makes sure to get enough rest. His life has changed for the better.

Continue to develop your skills and abilities. Learn as much as you can about yourself: the skills that you have and can develop; what you do well; and the type of work environment that is most conducive to your success. Be willing to move outside your comfort zone and try something different. Do not become stuck repeating actions that have not worked in the past. You will not get a better result.

This book is designed to be a resource that you can refer to again and again. The techniques that are described have helped others improve their performance and productivity. It is my sincere hope that they will do the same for you.

APPENDIX

ASPERGER'S SYNDROME GUIDE FOR EMPLOYERS

Barbara Bissonnette, Principal
Forward Motion Coaching[1]

Asperger's Syndrome is a mild form of autism that affects interpersonal communication and the ability to organize information and prioritize tasks. The individual may make blunt or inappropriate comments, and have difficulty multitasking and seeing the big picture. He or she may be unusually distracted by noise, smells or physical sensations. Each individual is unique and does not share all of the traits of Asperger's Syndrome or experience them to the same degree.

While these individuals face a number of challenges, Asperger's Syndrome also confers specific strengths that make them particularly well suited to jobs requiring attention to detail and prolonged focus. Many have above-average intelligence and enter the workforce with advanced or multiple college degrees. Although represented in all types of jobs and careers, the fields of computer technology, academic and scientific research, writing, engineering, technical documentation, and academia make particularly good use of their logic and analytical skills.

The business community is beginning to recognize that people with Asperger's Syndrome can be terrific assets when they are in the right jobs, and receive the needed supports. Specialisterne is a software testing company, founded in Denmark, that specifically hires individuals with Asperger's Syndrome and high-functioning autism. Its clients include Microsoft and Oracle. According to founder Thorkil Sonne, these individuals make superior software testers because, "…they are methodical and exhibit great attention

---

1   Excerpted from *Asperger's Syndrome Workplace Survival Guide: A Neurotypical's Secrets for Success* © Barbara Bissonnette 2013.

to detail," and have "motivation, focus, persistence, precision and ability to follow instructions" (Sonne in Saran 2008).

Specialisterne is expanding operations throughout Europe, and in 2012 entered the United States. Thorkil Sonne established The Specialist People Foundation with the goal of creating one million jobs around the world for "specialist people" with autism and similar challenges. (To learn more, visit www.specialisterne.com.) Currently, Specialisterne has operations in Austria, Denmark, Iceland, Norway, Poland, Switzerland, the United Kingdom and the United States. Plans are underway for Canada, Germany, Singapore, Spain, and Turkey. Other organizations in the United States have adapted this model, including Aspiritech (www.aspiritech.org); and Semperical (www.semperical.com).

The strengths of individuals with Asperger's Syndrome include:

- Attention to detail and sustained concentration.

  Benefits: ability to spot errors; accuracy; not distracted from the task at hand.

- Excellent long-term memory.

  Benefits: recall facts and details others have forgotten.

- Tolerance of repetition and routine.

  Benefits: perform the same tasks without getting bored or burned out.

- Strong logic and analytic skills.

  Benefits: ability to see patterns/connections in data; objective view of the facts.

- Vast knowledge of specialized fields.

  Benefits: develop in-depth knowledge and expertise.

- Creative thinking.

  Benefits: different way of processing information can lead to novel solutions.

- Perseverance.

  Benefits: stick with a job until it is done.

- Honesty and loyalty.

  Benefits: not afraid to tell the truth; stay with an employer long term.

COMMON WORKPLACE CHALLENGES

Individuals with Asperger's Syndrome vary widely in their abilities, challenges and need of support. Some appear awkward in their interactions with others, forgetting to make eye contact or to smile, or talking too loudly, softly or quickly. Others are charming and talkative, but may ask too many questions, or alienate others with quirky behavior or unintentional social gaffes.

Workplace challenges fall into three primary categories: interpersonal communication, planning and organization, and sensory/motor difficulties. Communication deficits typically present the biggest hurdle, since they may appear to be attitude or behavior problems.

COMMUNICATION CHALLENGES

Figuring out what the social rules are depends on the context of a particular situation, and the type of relationship you have with the person to whom you are speaking. To the degree that an individual has trouble grasping situational context, he will struggle to say and do the "right" things. It is also important to understand your audience—that others have thoughts, desires, knowledge and motives that differ from your own. This "theory of mind" ability means that you can predict how someone is likely to react to a situation, and what he expects you to do.

The ability to infer another's emotional state is another component of effective communication. This information is often communicated nonverbally, through a person's facial expression, body language, and tone and volume of voice. Research has shown that only 7 percent of what people communicate about their attitudes and feelings comes from their spoken words. The vast majority—93 percent—comes from facial expression and the way that words are spoken (Mehrabian 1981).

Many individuals with Asperger's Syndrome have trouble noticing and/or interpreting nonverbal signals. They may not realize that someone is upset with them, or understand an implied request from a supervisor. They may not understand jokes or sarcasm.

Additionally, individuals may not be aware of the nonverbal messages *they* are sending by not making eye contact, standing too close to others, or speaking in a monotone.

Difficulty with social skills and interpersonal communication can cause people with Asperger's Syndrome to behave in ways that seem willfully rude or insubordinate. They may offend others with candid remarks, which they consider to be honest and factual. The literal interpretation of language can lead to serious, sometimes comical, misunderstandings: "How come you're not using the new scheduling software?" asks Kevin's manager, "I told you to take a look at it two weeks ago." "I *did* look at it," replies Kevin, "and didn't think it was useful so I deleted it off my system."

Unlike most people, who can subconsciously process contextual clues within a fraction of a second, individuals with Asperger's Syndrome must consciously notice and put the clues together. This takes time and mental effort (Vermeulen 2012). These individuals may not be able to figure out another person's motive, or know what is expected, based on inferences and previous experience, in time to react to the situation. Things that are obvious to most people are not obvious to Aspergians.

Common communication challenges:

- literal interpretation of language, misses implied meaning or sarcasm

- too honest and direct, unintentionally offending others

- neglecting to make eye contact or to smile (even though the individual is friendly)

- doesn't know how to engage with co-workers (e.g. make small talk)

- talks at length about areas of interest; doesn't notice that others want to end the conversation

- speaks to a supervisor in the same way he speaks to a peer

- interrupts, because he can't tell when someone is done speaking, or doesn't want to forget a point

- speaks too quickly or slowly; too loudly or softly

- ends conversations by simply walking away.

It must be stressed that these individuals *want* to interact with others, and are often surprised to hear that they have offended someone.

ORGANIZATIONAL CHALLENGES

Executive function refers to a broad array of cognitive processes needed for the effective management of time and resources. These processes serve as an "inner CEO," enabling an individual to establish goals and a realistic plan to achieve them; prioritize tasks; see options; monitor progress; and change course, if needed. Multitasking requires strong working memory, which is one of the executive functions. The ability to shift between the big picture and the relevant details is another.

Asperger's Syndrome can impact executive functioning in various ways. The employee may not see how his tasks fit into the larger whole, unless this is explicitly explained. He may need assistance to establish priorities, and utilize written notes and checklists in order to remember multistep processes (Meltzer 2010). Co-workers, who are aware of the person's talent and intellect, may brush aside appeals for help with comments like, "You should know what to do; it's obvious!" or, "At your level, you should know what the priorities are."

Common organizational challenges:

- not knowing how to begin an assignment

- difficulty estimating how long a project will or should take

- too much focus on details; loses sight of the purpose of a task

- unsure of what the finished product should look like

- forgets verbal instructions

- needs help prioritizing tasks

- difficulty with multitasking and frequent interruptions

- appearing not to take initiative, because next steps aren't clear

- asks too many questions, in an attempt to clarify assignments or expectations

- acts impulsively, or based on too little information.

SENSORY AND MOTOR CHALLENGES

Many individuals with Asperger's Syndrome experience hyper- or hypo-sensitivity to various sensory stimuli, and for some, this can interfere with job performance. The person may be able to see the cycling of fluorescent lights, or hear the sound of a co-worker's typing as a cacophony of utterly distracting noise. The smell of tobacco smoke on a colleague's clothing made one woman so ill that she had to quit her job.

It may be difficult or impossible to pay attention to input from multiple sensory channels at once. The person may not be able to look someone in the eye, *and* listen to what they are saying; or speak with a customer while simultaneously typing information into a computer database. Auditory processing problems can make it particularly difficult to follow group conversations.

Motor (muscle) problems are evidenced by messy or illegible handwriting, or an inability to write quickly enough to take notes during meetings. The person may find it difficult to fold and stuff papers neatly into envelopes. He might be clumsy or have an awkward gait.

Common sensory and motor challenges:

- over- or under-sensitive to noise, light, odors, and tactile sensations

- difficulty integrating stimulus from multiple sensory channels (e.g. cannot listen and look at someone simultaneously)

- may experience sensory overload and require a break

- not able to interpret group conversations

- difficulty with fine or gross muscle movement (e.g. difficulty with intricate tasks, poor coordination).

OPTIMAL JOBS AND WORK ENVIRONMENTS

Asperger's Syndrome exists on a spectrum and individuals can vary widely in their abilities and challenges. There is no "short list" of suitable jobs or careers. These individuals are represented in all types of occupations, as evidenced by this sampling of Forward Motion Coaching clients: technical writer, creative writer, editor, production manager, graphic artist, fine artist, teacher (toddlers to graduate students), physicist, project manager, sales manager, consultant, computer programmer/other IT, engineer, analyst, actuary, accountant, lawyer, paralegal, administrative assistant, retail sales associate, warehouse worker, electrician, physician, nurse, librarian, library clerk, and meteorologist!

However, generalities can be made about the type of jobs and work environments that are most conducive to their success:

- allow concentration on one task at a time

- favor accuracy and quality over speed

- offer structure and clear performance expectations

- have at least some elements of routine

- emphasize technical tasks and facts and information

- do not involve the management of others or sophisticated levels of interpersonal communication.

WORKING WITH PEOPLE WHO HAVE ASPERGER'S SYNDROME

There are many things that employers can do to help individuals with Asperger's Syndrome to be productive and successful at their jobs. If you know or suspect that someone has Asperger's Syndrome:

- Be patient during training, and break instruction into small segments. If an individual is asking an excessive number of questions, it could indicate anxiety or confusion about an assignment.

- Explain how tasks and assignments fit into the whole (the "big picture") and why particular steps or processes are important.

- Whenever possible, encourage the use of written notes, outlines, and checklists. Icons and color-coded filing systems will help with organization. People with Asperger's Syndrome are usually visual, not auditory, learners.

- Assist the individual with creating a personalized "rule book" that contains processes, procedures, and where to go for help.

- Check for understanding by asking the individual to summarize an assignment.

- Make expectations specific and quantifiable: "The draft is due in three days, and should include at least six ideas for improving efficiency" or "Thirty entries or more must be made per hour." Avoid vague, abstract directives: "Take the data and run with it" or "I want you to take ownership of the project."

- If there is a performance problem, bring it to the individual's attention using clear, explicit language. Hints, inferences, and sarcasm will not be understood. Be direct: "You must limit emails to four paragraphs;"

or "There is too much detail in this presentation, what I need is…" or "The priority is to complete the data entry by noon."

- Be mindful that *what looks like a behavior or attitude problem is usually a communication problem.* Don't take blunt remarks or social gaffes personally. Clarify the individual's intentions. Be specific and matter-of-fact in pointing out inappropriate or unacceptable behavior. General statements such as "You're rude;" or "You're not a team player;" or "How could you say that?!" are confusing. Be direct: "When you tell people to 'be quiet' it's considered rude. Instead, ask them to lower their voices."

- Assign a "work buddy" or mentor to explain social norms, encourage social interaction, and answer questions. Individuals with Asperger's Syndrome often hesitate to ask questions, fearing that they will appear "stupid," or that the wrong question will result in job loss.

- Relax the standards for "teamwork" where possible, and allow these individuals to focus on the technical aspects of the job.

- Take sensory difficulties seriously. An individual who is hyper-sensitive to noise may require a quiet workspace, noise-cancelling headphones, or a white noise machine. Someone with an auditory processing problem may need to use a TTY (text telephone) or other assistive technology. A photo sensitivity can be mitigated by a natural light source, or lamps with incandescent light bulbs.

  Olfactory sensitivities can be addressed by the use of personal air fresheners in the workspace. Consider limiting the consumption of food to the lunch room.

- Give an individual permission to take short breaks in order to avoid sensory overload.

- These individuals often experience heightened levels of anxiety, and as a result may magnify a situation. They may panic over a minor mistake, or an insignificant disagreement with a co-worker. Often, they do not know how to correct the situation. Do not dismiss concerns as trivial, or something that the individual should know how to handle. Listen, acknowledge concerns, and brainstorm an action plan.

- Educate human resources personnel, managers and employees about Asperger's Syndrome. Increased understanding is directly proportional to increased employment success. Retaining just one employee at risk of derailing more than covers the investment in training.

- Provide a coach who is familiar with conditions like Asperger's Syndrome to work with an employee and his or her manager. The pragmatic, goal-oriented nature of the coaching, combined with an action plan based on organizational needs, assures that performance objectives are addressed. (Although in most cases it is illegal, under the Americans with Disabilities Act, to ask an employee about a disability, you *can* discuss performance issues. Readers outside the U.S. should consult their local laws regarding discrimination.)

REFERENCES

American Psychiatric Association (2000) *Diagnostic and Statistical Manual of Mental Disorders (DSM-IV-TR)*. Arlington: American Psychiatric Publishing, Inc.

Attwood, T. (2007) *The Complete Guide to Asperger's Syndrome*. London: Jessica Kingsley Publishers.

Bornstein, D. (2011) "For Some with Autism, Jobs to Match their Talents," Opinionator blog, *The New York Times*, 30 June. Available at http://opinionator.blogs.nytimes.com/2011/06/30/putting-the-gifts-of-the-autistic-to-work, accessed on 4 February 2013.

Burns, D.D. (1980, 1999) *Feeling Good: The New Mood Therapy*. New York: Avon Books, an imprint of HarperCollins Publishers.

Canadian Centre for Occupational Health and Safety (2005) *Bullying in the Workplace*. Available at www.ccohs.ca/oshanswers/psychosocial/bullying.html, accessed on 23 December 2012.

CareerBuilder (2012) "CareerBuilder Study Finds More Workers Feeling Bullied in the Workplace." Available at www.careerbuilder.com/share/aboutus/pressreleasesdetail.aspx?sd=8/29/2012&sc_cmp1=cb_pr713_&siteid=cbpr&id=pr713&ed=12/31/2012, accessed on 4 February 2013.

Clark, K. (2012) *The Healthy Workplace Bill* (House Bill 2310/Senate Bill S 916). Personal correspondence, October 2012.

Cobb, E.P. (2012) *Workplace Bullying: A Global Health and Safety Issue*. Boston, MA: The Isosceles Group. Available at http://ilera2012.wharton.upenn.edu/refereedpapers/cobbellen.pdf, accessed on 21 December 2012.

Cooper-Kahn, J. and Dietzel, L. (2008) *Late, Lost, and Unprepared*. Bethesda, MD; Woodbine House, Inc.

Farr, M. and Shatkin, L. (2009) *300 Best Jobs Without a Four-Year Degree*. Indianapolis, IN; JIST Publishing.

Fast, Y. (2004) *Employment for Individuals with Asperger Syndrome or Non-Verbal Learning Disability*. London: Jessica Kingsley Publishers.

Fogle, P.T. (2013) *Essentials of Communication Sciences and Disorders*. Clifton Park, NY: Delmar, Cengage Learning.

Gabor, D. (1983, 2001) *How to Start a Conversation and Make Friends, Revised and Updated*. New York: Fireside.

Gathercole, S.E. and Alloway, T.P. (2008) *Working Memory and Learning*. London: Sage Publications Ltd.

Gebelein, S.H., Lee, D.G., Nelson-Neuhaus, K.J. and Sloan, E.B. (1996, 1999) *Successful Executive's Handbook*. Minneapolis, MN: ePredix.

Goleman, D. (1998) *Working with Emotional Intelligence*. New York, NY: Bantam Books.

Harmon, A. (2011) "Autistic and Seeking a Place in an Adult World." *The New York Times*, 17 September.

Holmes, T.H. and Rahe, R.H. (1967) "The social readjustment rating scale." *Journal of Psychosomatic Research 11*, 2, 213–18.

Job Accommodation Network (2005, latest update 2011) *Workplace Accommodations: Low Cost, High Impact*. Available at http://AskJAN.org/media/LowCostHighImpact.doc, accessed on 9 June 2012.

Johnson, S. (2003) "Emotions and the Brain: Fear." *Discover Magazine,* March 2003. Available at http://discovermagazine.com/2003/mar/cover, accessed on 26 October 2012. Copyright © 2012 Kalmbach Publishing Company.

Lewis, M. (2010) *The Big Short: Inside the Doomsday Machine*. Excerpted in "Betting on the Blind Side." *Vanity Fair*, No. 596, April. New York: Conde Nast.

Mehrabian, A. (1981) *Silent Messages: Implicit Communication of Emotions and Attitudes*. Belmont, CA: Wadsworth (currently being distributed by Albert Mehrabian, am@kaaj.com).

Meltzer, L. (2007) *Executive Function in Education from Theory to Practice*. New York: The Guilford Press.

Meltzer, L. (2010) *Promoting Executive Function in the Classroom*. New York: The Guilford Press.

Myles, B. *et al.* (2000) *Asperger Syndrome and Sensory Issues*. Shawnee Mission, KS: Autism Asperger Publishing Company.

NACE (2011) *Job Outlook 2012*. Bethlehem, PA: National Association of Colleges and Employers (NACE).

Palladino, L.J. (2007) *Find Your Focus Zone*. New York: Free Press division of Simon & Schuster, Inc.

Peltier, B. (2001) *The Psychology of Executive Coaching, Theory and Application*. New York: Taylor & Francis.

Saran, C. (2008) "Specialisterne finds a place in workforce for people with autism." ComputerWeekly. com, February 8. Reed Business Information.

Shatkin, L. and the Editors at JIST (2008) *200 Best Jobs for Introverts*. Indianapolis, IN: JIST Publishing.

Tileston, D.W. (2004) *What Every Teacher Should Know About Learning, Memory, and the Brain*. Thousand Oaks, CA: Corwin Press.

U.S. Equal Employment Opportunity Commission (2012a) *Harassment*. Available at www.eeoc.gov/laws/practices/harassment.cfm, accessed on 1 February 2013.

U.S. Equal Employment Opportunity Commission (2012b) *Disability Discrimination & Harassment*. Available at www.eeoc.gov/laws/types/disability.cfm, accessed on 1 February 2013.

Vermeulen, P. (2012) *Autism as Context Blindness*. Shawnee Mission, KS: Autism Asperger Publishing Company.

Winner, M.G. and Crooke, P. (2011) *Social Thinking at Work, Why Should I Care?* San Jose, CA: Think Social Publishing, Inc.

Workplace Bullying Institute (2012) Bellingham, WA. See www.workplacebullying.org, accessed on 10 November 2012.

Young, K.S. and Travis, H.P. (2008) *Communicating Nonverbally, A Practical Guide to Presenting Yourself More Effectively*. Long Grove, IL; Waveland Press, Inc.

FURTHER READING

Austin, R.D., Wareham, J. and Busquets, J. (2008) "Specialisterne: Sense & Details," *Harvard Business Review,* February. Harvard Business School Press, President and Fellows of Harvard College.

Dubin, N. (2009) *Asperger Syndrome and Anxiety, A Guide to Successful Stress Management.* London: Jessica Kingsley Publishers.

Gaus, V.L. (2007) *Cognitive-Behavioral Therapy for Adult Asperger Syndrome.* New York: The Guilford Press.

Grandin, T. and Barron, S. (2005) *Unwritten Rules of Social Relationships, Decoding Social Mysteries Through the Unique Perspective of Autism.* Arlington, TX: Future Horizons, Inc.

Grandin, T. and Duffy, K. (2008) *Developing Talents, Careers for Individuals with Asperger Syndrome and High-Functioning Autism.* Updated, expanded edition. Shawnee Mission, KS: Autism Asperger Publishing Company.

McIntyre, M.G. (2005) *Secrets to Winning at Office Politics.* New York: St. Martin's Press.

Ward, S. (2009) "How to Teach Executive Function Skills at Home." Lincoln, MA: The Center for Executive Function Skill Development. Seminar, May.

Zaks, Z. (2006) *Life and Love: Positive Strategies for Autistic Adults.* Shawnee Mission, KS: Autism Asperger Publishing Company.

ABOUT THE AUTHOR

Barbara Bissonnette is a certified coach and the Principal of Forward Motion Coaching (www.forwardmotion.info). She specializes in career development coaching and workplace advocacy for individuals with Asperger's Syndrome and Nonverbal Learning Disorder (NLD). She also provides training and consultations to organizations on how to utilize the skills of employees with communication and executive function challenges.

Prior to coaching, Barbara spent more than 20 years in business, most recently as Vice President of Marketing and Sales for an information services company. She has experience hiring and managing people at all levels. She also understands the challenges of Asperger's Syndrome and NLD and focuses on practical strategies for employment success.

Barbara earned a graduate certificate in Executive Coaching from the Massachusetts School of Professional Psychology and is certified by the Institute for Professional Empowerment Coaching. She and her husband live in Massachusetts.

INDEX

$20 words 102
200 Best Jobs for Introverts (Shatkin) 152
300 Best Jobs Without a Four-Year Degree (Farr and Shatkin) 152
360-degree feedback 62

accepting your limitations 145–6
accommodations
    examples 173–4
    limits to 174
    negotiating 176
    overview 173
    for sensory issues 131–2
accountability 113
action inhibitors 110
action plans 110–14
    example 113–14
    flexibility 113
    template 111–12
adjusting behavior 24
advice, asking for 54
Alloway, T.P. 88
Americans with Disabilities Act (ADA) 172–5, 199
amygdala 116–17
amygdala hijack 116, 117
anxiety 43, 198
    management 125–30
    positive self-talk 129–30
    reframing 129
    riding the wave 129
    triggers 125–6
arrogance 58
artifacts 26
asking for advice 54
asking for help 43–5
asking questions 43–5
asking the right person 44, 45
Asperger's Syndrome, understanding of 16
Aspiritech 189, 192
assessing situations 23

assistive technology 132–3
assumptions 126–7, 128
    of neurotypicals 23
Attwood, Tony 116–17
auditory learners 56
auditory processing 195–6, 198
authority
    dealing with 65–8
    overstepping 74–5
    sources of 80
Autism as Context Blindness (Vermeulen) 23
autism spectrum disorders, in workplace 188

behavior, adjusting 24
being helpful 45–6
being positive 32
black and-white thinking 129
body language *see* nonverbal communication
book, overview and how to use 17–19
boredom 167
Bornstein, D. 189
brainstorming 52–3
building on strengths 142–5
building relationships 40
    reciprocating 42
bullying and harassment 134–40
    avoiding 140
    company procedures 139
    effects of 135
    legal action 140
    legislation 135–8
    prevalence 134
    reporting 139–40
    types of 134–5
    what to do 138–40
Burns, David 120–1
Burry, Michael 143

career management
    accepting limitations 145–6

being a manager 152–4
building on strengths 142–5
developing skills and talents 144–5
elevator speeches 164–5
getting fired 165–9, 187
networking 160–2, 163–4
overview 141–2
professional associations 162–3
resignation 167, 169–71
SWOT analysis 155–9
wrong job or career 150–2
CareerBuilder® 134, 135
catastrophizing 120
chains of command, official and unofficial 80
challenging 67
change 68–72
    adapting to 72
    fear of 70–1
    resisting 69
    signs of 69–70
    thinking patterns 122–5
    willingness for 19
changing perceptions 53
Checklist of Common Workplace Challenges 145–9
checklists 89
choices 106
chronemics 26
chunking information 89
clarifying expectations 53–6
Clark, Katherine 136
clothing 134
coaching 199
    principles of 15–16
Cobb, E.P. 134, 135
cognitive distortion 120–1
comments, constructive vs. combative 71
communication
    audience and context 101

challenges 193–4
choice of words 102
choosing medium 103
editing 102–3
effective 100–3
emotional component 24
ending conversations 28
getting to the point 100–3
importance 21
improving 166–7
meaning and context 22–5
nonverbal 25–9
overview 20–1
planning messages 100–1
situational clues 23
company culture 40
company policies and rules,
    sticking to 46
complaining 32
compliments, receiving 35
compromise 55
confidence 57–60
conflict with authority 66–7
conflicts
    and disagreements 72–7
    and misunderstandings 77–8
context 24–5
    of communication 23
    nonverbal communication 28
    putting things in 77–8
conversations, not interrupting
    32–3
Cooper-Kahn, J. 87
corporate culture 79–80
criticism, accepting and using
    62–4
criticizing others 64–5
Crooke, Pamela 29
cultural expectations, fitting with
    16–17
cultures, within businesses 78–9

Daily Activity Log 90–2
dandelion philosophy 189
dealing with authority 65–8
dealing with change 68–72
decision-making 104–5
    in management 154
deference, to bosses 67–8
departmental cultures 79
depression 121, 128
diet 130
Dietzel, L. 87
difficult bosses 66
disability-related questions
    174–5

disagreeing, use of language 75
disagreements, and conflicts 72–7
disclosure 14, 131
    confidentiality 185
    deciding whether to disclose
        172–3
    dos and don'ts 183–5
    including strengths 184–5
    during job interviews 178–9
    at job offer 179
    legal aspects 175
    purpose of 179
    solution-focused 175–80
    after starting work 179–80
    strategies 176, 185–7
    timing of 177–80
    when applying for jobs 177–8
disclosure need and action scale
    181–2
discrimination 172–5
    protection for employers 174
    risk of 14
dismissal 165–9, 187
disqualifying positives 121
distractions, dealing with 88–9
dress and grooming 32, 134
    confidence 59

editing, communication 102–3
education, of co-workers 199
efficiency, improving 93
electronic devices, for self-
    organizing 89
elevator speeches 164–5
emails
    checking 88–9
    wise use of 102
emotion management
    anxiety management 125–30
    anxiety triggers 125–6
    behaviors to avoid 115–16
    bullying and harassment
        134–40
    changing thinking patterns
        122–5
    and job retention 166–7
    meltdowns 116–17
    overview 115
    positive self-talk 129–30
    putting other people's actions
        into perspective 119–21
    realistic expectations 130
    reframing 129
    riding the wave 129
    self-awareness 117–18
    sensory issues 130–4

stress 117–19
    trigger factors 117–18
emotional reasoning 121
emotions
    and communication 24
    getting fired 166, 168–9
    recognizing 115
employer expectations 49–53
    clarifying 53–6
employer guidelines, working
    to 55
employment readiness 49
employment statistics 13
ending conversations 28
enemies, supervisors as 67
Equal Employment Opportunity
    Commission (U.S.) 136–7,
    140, 169
executive functioning 194–5
    action plans 110–14
    communication 100–3
    flexibility 103–6
    goal setting 106–9
    project planning 94–9
    time management 86–7, 89–93
    working memory 87–9
exercise 118, 130
expectations
    clarifying 53–6
    meeting 49–53, 168
    realistic 130
    understanding 168
    unrealistic 74
experimentation 19
explanatory statements 183

Farr, M. 152
Fast, Y. 138
feedback
    accepting and using 62–4
    asking for 54–5
    giving 75–6
    understanding 51
    work buddies 42
*Feeling Good: The New Mood
    Therapy* (Burns) 120–1
filtering 121
Find Your Focus Zone (Palladino)
    87, 113, 139
finding out 44
first impressions
    importance of 30
    meeting new people 33–4
    positive 31–3
    small talk 34–7
    welcome lunches 37–40

fitting in 78, 83
    elements of 30–1
flexibility 103–6
    action plans 113
Fogle, P.T. 22
following instructions 31
fortune telling 121
friction, between co-workers
    73–4
friendliness 35

Gabor, Don 37
Gathercole, S.E. 88
Gebelein, S.H. 58
getting to the point 100–3
goal setting 106–9
goals 19
    meaningful 110
    positive self-talk 130
    realistic 58
    template 111–12
Goleman, Daniel 116, 117
grayscale thinking 106
grooming and dress 32
guide for employers 191–9

habits, changing 93
handshakes 133–4
harassment and bullying 134–40
    avoiding 140
    company procedures 139
    effects of 135
    legal action 140
    legislation 135–8
    prevalence 134
    reporting 139–40
    types of 134–5
    what to do 138–40
harassment, definition 136–7
headphones, noise cancelling
    132
health and safety 174–5
Healthy Workplace Bill 135–6
help/advice, office politics 84
helpfulness 45–6
Holmes, T.H. 165
*How to Start a Conversation and
    Make Friends* (Gabor) 37
humor 44
hypersensitivity 131, 195–6, 198
hyposensitivity 131, 195–6

Information, Preparation,
    Practice model 127
information processing speed
    145

inhibition 87
instructions 54
intellectual superiority 66–7
interactions 74
interpersonal relationships,
    importance 20–1
interrupting 32–3
interruptions 88
introductions 33–4
Irlen Method 132

Job Accommodation Network
    (JAN) 175, 178
job interviews, positive self-talk
    130
job loss 165–9, 187
job readiness 174
job seeking
    elevator speeches 164–5
    networking 160–2, 163–4
job types 196–7
Johnson, S. 116
jumping to conclusions 121

keeping in touch 161
keeping notes 44
kinesthetic learners 56

labeling 121
language
    confidence 59
    neutral 75
learning how things are done
    31, 40–1
    office politics 84–5
learning styles 56
legal action, bullying and
    harassment 140
legislation
    anti-discrimination 172–5
    bullying and harassment
        135–8
    people with disabilities 137,
        172–5, 199
Lewis, Michael 143
limitations, accepting 145–6
LinkedIn 162
listening 32–3, 49–50
lunches, joining in 83

management
    features of role 154
    moving into 152–4
    of people who have Asperger's
        197–9

Massachusetts, Healthy
    Workplace Bill 136
medical professionals, consulting
    118, 128, 130
meditation 118
meeting new people 33–4
Mehrabian, A. 26, 193–4
meltdowns 116–17
Meltzer, L. 88, 108, 195
mentors 41, 113
mind reading 121
miscommunication 22
misinterpreting an action or
    remark 77
misunderstandings 77–8
mnemonics 89
motivation 19, 110, 113
    lack of 167
    and rewards 114
motor challenges 195–6
multitasking 88, 195
Myles, B. 131

Namie, Gary 135
negative assumptions 126–7,
    128
negative thinking 120–1
    changing 122–5
networking 160–2, 163–4
neuropsychological evaluation
    152
neurotypicals
    assumptions of 23
    social orientation 74, 78
neutral language 75
noise cancelling headphones 132
non-judgmental feedback 75–6
nonverbal communication 25–9,
    193
    confidence 58
    context 28
    observation 28, 101
    practicing 28
    self-awareness 28
    understanding of 28–9
norms, fitting with 16–17
note-keeping 44, 54, 89
NT Tips
    allowing extra time 95
    being in the wrong job 55
    dealing with authority 67
    eavesdropping 46
    ending conversations 28
    fitting in 83
    focusing 113
    food smells 133

How to Start a Conversation and Make Friends (Gabor) 37
interruptions 88
motivation and rewards 114
professional associations 69–70
receiving compliments 35
sincerity 76
Social Thinking® 28
welcome lunches 39

observation
nonverbal communication 28
office politics 84
observing co-workers 54
Occupational Outlook Handbook 152
office politics 78–80
in action 80–5
dealing with the bad stuff 85
olfactory sensitivities 133, 198
online business networking 162
options 103–6
organizational challenges 194–5
organizational culture 78–80
orientations, neurotypicals and Aspergians 20
other people's actions, putting into perspective 119–21
overcommunication 100–1
overgeneralization 121
overreaction 138–9
overstepping authority 74–5

Palladino, Lucy Jo 87, 113, 139
paralanguage 26
past tense, use of 28
Peltier, B. 129
people skills 49
accepting feedback/criticism 62–4
criticizing others 64–5
dealing with authority 65–8
dealing with change 68–72
problem areas 61–2
perceptions, changing 53
perfection 59
performance 49
perks 80
personal hygiene 133
personal limitations, accepting 145–6
personalization 119–20, 121
perspectives
other peoples' 24–5
putting things into 77–8

photo sensitivity 198
planning, and time management 89–90
planning projects 94–9
polarized thinking 120
positive self-talk 129–30
power, knowing who has 80
practice 59–60
to reduce anxiety 127
pragmatic ability 22
pragmatics 22, 24–5
preparation, to reduce anxiety 127
prioritizing 41, 49
probationary status 30
problem-solving 51–3
problems, positive self-talk 130
processing speed 145
procrastination 89
professional associations 69–70, 144–5, 162–3
project planning 94–9
projecting confidence 57–60
purpose of your work 53–4

questioning and challenging 67

Rahe, R.H. 165
Rationality of Beliefs Checklist 122–4
reacting to requests 68
reality checks 42
reframing 129
relationship building 40
reciprocating 42
relaxation, positive self-talk 130
resignation 167, 169–71
sample letter 171
responsibilities, keeping to 31
rewards, for achievement 114
riding the wave 129
rigidity 150
routines 89
rudeness 13, 35, 36, 45, 46, 53, 193–4
rumors 70

sarcasm 44
Scion Capital 143
scripts 21
seeing the big picture 23, 45, 47, 50–1
self-awareness
emotion management 117–18
nonverbal communication 28
self-confidence 57–60

self-doubt 57
Semperical 189, 192
sensory issues 130–4, 195–6, 198
accommodations for 131–2
sensory integration and assistive technologies 132–3
sensory processing 131
shaking hands 34, 133–4
Shatkin, L. 152
shortcuts 93
shoulds 120
signs of problems, missing 167
Silent Messages (Mehrabian) 26
situational clues, for communication 23
sizing up, people and situations 23
skill development 144–5
small talk 34–7
examples 36–7
SMART goals 107–9
smiling 33–4
social orientation, neurotypicals 74, 78
Social Thinking at Work, Why Should I Care? (Winner and Crooke) 29
Social Thinking® 29
solution-focused disclosure 175–80
Sonne, Thorkil 143, 188, 189, 191–2
Specialist People Foundation 143, 188, 192
Specialisterne 143, 188, 191
stereotypes 16
Stern, Lewis 122–4
Story, Ellen 136
strengths
building on 142–5
people with Asperger's 192
profiling 144
stress, recognition and management 117–19
success 59
summarizing 54
supervisors, asking what they want 54
SWOT analysis 155–9

tactile learners 56
tactile sensitivities 133
taking things personally 77, 119–20, 121

talents, development 144–5
tasks, rating importance of 90
team work 46–9, 198, 20–1
templates
    Daily Activity Log 91–2
    disclosure need and action
        scale 181–2
    project planning 98–9
    SMART goals 109
    weekly goals and action items
        111–12
*The Complete Guide to Asperger's
    Syndrome* (Attwood)
    116–17
*The Psychology of Executive
    Coaching, Theory and
    Application* (Peltier) 129
theory of mind 24
thinking patterns
    black and-white thinking 129
    changing 122–5
time management 86–7, 89–93
    estimating time needed 93
time, use of 26
timekeeping 32
timing 86–7
    giving feedback 75–6
trainers 41
transferable skills 151–2
Travis, H.P. 26
triggers
    of anxiety 125–6
    of emotional arousal 117–18

understanding the job 50–1,
    53–4
U.S. Department of Labor 152

values 79
Vermeulen, Peter 23, 24, 194
viewpoints, seeing other peoples'
    24–5
visual learners 56
voicemail checking 88–9

welcome lunches 37–40
white noise 132
Winner, Michelle Garcia 29
work buddies 40–2, 198
    choosing 42
    reciprocating 42
working environment 196–7
    as group endeavor 21
    problems of 13–14
working memory 87–9, 145,
    195

Workplace Bullying Institute
    134, 135
workplace challenges 193–6
written instructions 54
wrong job or career 150–2

Young, K.S. 26